California Wild Lands

California Wild Lands

A GUIDE TO THE NATURE CONSERVANCY PRESERVES

DWIGHT HOLING

CHRONICLE BOOKS • SAN FRANCISCO

Printed in the United States of America.

Library of Congress Cataloging in Publication Data:

Holing, Dwight.
  California wild lands.

  Includes index.
  1. Natural areas — California — Guide-books.   2. Nature Conservancy (U.S.)   I. Title.
QH476.5.C2H65   1988
333.95′09794   87-32545
ISBN 0-87701-497-3 (pbk.)

Editor: Frankie Wright
Design by: Seventeenth Street Studios
Composition: TBH/Typecast, Inc.

Photo credits:

Tom Hesseldenz, p. 12; Sue Van Hook, p. 22; Laure Oliver, p. 29; Hella Hammid, pps. 35, 121, 178; Pat Lisser, p. 41; Jerry Ott, p. 47; Ken Reichard, p. 54; Daniel D'Agostini, p. 64; Steve McCormick, p. 72; Mark Citret, p. 92; Debra Hansen, p. 98; Tom Griggs, p. 104; Saxon Holt, p. 111; Bev Steveson, p. 138; Pacific Western Aerial Surveys, p. 146; Lynn Learned, p. 155; George Helmkamp, p. 160.

Illustration credits:

Keith Hansen, pages 33, 70, 126, 135, 153, 161, 167.
Andrea Pickart, pages 19, 26, 37, 42, 60, 73, 78, 93, 109, 112, 144, 147, 176.
Maps by Eureka Cartography

Grateful acknowledgement is made to Random House for permission to reprint copyrighted material on page 89: excerpts from "Meditation on Saviors" and "The Answer" from *The Selected Poetry of Robinson Jeffers*.

Distributed in Canada by Raincoast Books
112 East Third Avenue, Vancouver, B.C. V5T 1C8

10 9 8 7 6 5 4 3 2 1

Chronicle Books
San Francisco, California

Contents

Section 3: South

Acknowledgments

This book would have been impossible to write without the assistance and guidance of the entire staff at The Nature Conservancy's California Field Office in San Francisco. I am especially indebted to Will Murray, membership coordinator. Will helped conceptualize the project and brought it to life. He was instrumental in every phase, from coordinating the visuals with the text to tracking down the Latin and the common species names for the appendix. He sweated out the deadlines with me, gave invaluable scientific expertise, helped with the wordsmithing, and provided encouragement along the way. I also owe a tremendous thanks to all the preserve managers and volunteers who acted as my guides during site reconnaissance and who later reviewed the text for factual accuracy. Thanks also to Kim Nabi for help with the appendix; Keith Hansen and Andrea Pickart for drawings; John Parsons of Eureka Cartography; Frankie Wright for editing; Alison Silverstein; and the many photographers whose works grace these pages. Special appreciation goes to my parents, John and Patricia, for their faith and support, and to my wife, Ann Notthoff, and my children, Mary and Sam, for indulging my peregrinations. And last, I'd like to acknowledge the 1987 San Francisco Giants; their exciting broadcasts enlivened many a drive up and down Interstate 5.

Foreword

California Riches

IT HAS always been the Golden State. Even before the legions of miners came streaming across the continent, gold has melded with the image of California.

For the American immigrants who struggled over the Sierra Nevada in the 1840s, gold was the color of the land they found. Dried grasses shone in golden vastness throughout the Great Central Valley and along the rolling hills above the coast. The deep gold of autumn's maple leaves, oak duff, and fallen pine needles carpeted the floors of foothill canyons. And in spring, after winter rains, poppy fields in bright gold bloomed and rebloomed, illuminating whole valleys.

But gold, of course, and the promises of riches beyond hope, burst from naturalistic image to tantalizing reality with a single discovery in 1848. Suddenly, in just seven years, the region's non-native population jumped from 7,000 to 224,000. And that did it. California became forever a land that would glitter and beckon—a land of hyperbole and, some say, excess.

The forty-niners had only begun their digging when the region's few scientists began to crow about the riches *they'd* unearthed. Meeting in San Francisco to found a research society, the California Academy of Sciences, the pioneering scholars recorded their astonishment at the "rare and rich productions" of nature they saw around them: "We have on this coast . . . a field of richer promise in the department of natural history in all its variety than has previously been discovered."

Theirs was a bold statement, a boast really, one that now seems perfectly characteristic of the time and place. But in the thirteen decades since the statement was issued, thousands of studies have proved that, if anything, the naturalists were understating their case. California, we have learned, has the greatest species richness, the greatest ecological diversity, and the highest rate of endemism of any region in the continental United States.

Species richness? An inventory of the state's rare plants puts it this way: "More than 5,000 plants are native, a number that is more than that for the entire northeastern U.S. and Canada, an area ten times larger than California."

As for ecological diversity, one can slice the pie many ways. Just to keep watch over the state's animals, for example, the Department of Fish and Game must recognize 178 *major* habitat types, from Coastal Salt Marsh to Alpine Fell Field. Staff of the California Natural Heritage Section (a state heritage program) cuts the pie more carefully and recognizes somewhere around three hundred natural communities. And as they look more closely, the number keeps going up.

Rate of endemism? At least a third of all the plants native to California are endemic — that is, they occur naturally nowhere else on earth. Among the animals, at least fifty percent of the combined totals of species and subspecies are not found outside the state. These endemics increasingly end up on the growing lists of rare and endangered species crying for protection.

If the people who drew the state boundaries had set out deliberately to create a unique and highly diverse republic of plants and animals, they could not have done a much better job. Natural and political borders traditionally carve right through the middles of watersheds. But in California, for a change something went right.

By accident as much as by design the state's founders, in a single act, circumscribed a terrain of enormous variety: four major mountain ranges (the highest reaching 14,000 feet), two watersheds, each larger than New Hampshire, innumerable rivers and lakes (including a couple of saline ones), a thousand miles of seacoast, several good-sized islands offshore, two dormant volcanoes, and large portions of three distinct deserts. Most important, they corralled almost all of a huge biotic assemblage that has since come to be called the California Floristic Province. This high-flown term is simply a botanist's name for the landscape most people envision when they think of wild California. Up north are the giant redwoods, hemmed in between the mountains and the coast; Yosemite Valley, Lake Tahoe, and the rest of John Muir's beloved Sierra Nevada dominate the east; in the middle is the Great Central Valley, once a vast sea of grasses and marshes, now mostly given over to agriculture; and in the south are estuaries and the chaparral-covered mountains around Los Angeles and San Diego.

The province does, in fact, have clear natural boundaries. It is often described by the state's biologists as the part of California that's *cismontane,* meaning "on this side of the mountains." On the other side (*transmontane,* the experts say) is the rest of the nation, held at bay by the Great

Basin, and the Mojave and Colorado deserts. Within the California Floristic Province, the proportion of endemic plants has been calculated at more than forty-seven percent.

Isolated at the edge of the continent by mountains and deserts, California is in many ways an island, a world unto itself. This distinction alone would have given the state a good chance to develop its unusual flora and fauna, but California's fortuitous location within atmospheric currents greatly magnified the probabilities. California's climate, perhaps even more than its terrain, sets the region apart.

The climatic regime is straightforward. Winters are mild and wet; summers are warm and dry. So what? The regime itself is rare. California is the *only* region in North America that exhibits this pattern, and it's one of only a handful worldwide: the Mediterranean region, Chile, southwestern South Africa, and westernmost Australia. (All of these areas harbor large numbers of endemic species.)

Things become interesting when, inevitably, the climate and topography interact. In winter, globe-circling winds drive Pacific storms onto the land; where the storms meet the region's mountains, they drop their moisture, often in copious amounts. Parts of Northern California receive as many as 120 inches of rainfall a year.

Summer is vastly different. The summer rainstorms that regularly moisten Oregon and Washington, even sometimes drench Arizona and New Mexico, typically miss California altogether. From June to September most of the state desiccates under cloudless skies.

But different kinds of terrain are better at holding and releasing water. Further, some sites — deep canyons, north-facing slopes — receive less of the summer's relentless sunshine. Large areas, like those high in the Sierra Nevada, remain cool despite long exposure to intense solar radiation. Near the coast, summer fog and ocean breezes keep temperatures in the 60s and 70s, day and night, for months at a time. Other regions, such as Death Valley, may broil every day from April to October in temperatures of 100 degrees and up.

This interaction between climate and topography creates a staggering diversity of habitats — some continually and abundantly wet, some always dry; some freezing in winter and blazing in summer, others moderate and equable all year. The habitats shift and intergrade in a dizzyingly complex patchwork.

The patchiness of the state's habitat matrix is also a product of time and the earth's history, which have formed and reformed the terrain. During the 150 million years in which California has existed as part of North America, the region's changing assemblages of plants and animals have been subject to an intricate mix of influences: the rise and fall of sea level, the rapid growth and erosion of mountain ranges, the comings and goings of glaciers, the invasion and retreat of continental forests, the tectonic transport of whole chunks of the planet's surface, and the birth of numerous small pockets of unusual soils. Accordingly, many of the state's present endemic organisms, plants especially, are stragglers—relicts, in biologic lingo—that once enjoyed much more widespread distributions. Others are newcomers that have recently evolved to exploit narrow environmental conditions, such as the combination of severe summer drought and soils rich in toxic magnesium. In some cases, whole communities are distinctive, such as the local chaparrals composed of endemic plants like manzanita and Ione Buckwheat.

Cone Peak is the second highest peak in the Santa Lucia mountains, a remote coastal range that forms the craggy backbone of the Big Sur region. Although not one of California's tallest mountains, it has other virtues. Distributed in a loose collar around Cone Peak's summit is a stand of spire-shaped firs, their drooping branches bristling with stout, glossy needles. These are Santa Lucia Firs. The Cone Peak stand is small, just a couple of miles across, one of about a half dozen groves of similar size in the Santa Lucias. Except for scatterings of individuals surrounding the groves, this is it—the entire distribution of North America's rarest fir.

Cone Peak is also a remarkable biological vantage point. From the summit, looking thirty miles south along the Santa Lucia Range, one can see the upper watershed of a tiny stream called Salmon Creek. Here on a north-facing slope are the southernmost redwoods. From Salmon Creek all the way to Chetco Creek, just into Oregon 450 miles north, runs an intermittent strip of redwood forest—here thinning, there broadening, but always seaward of the crest of the coastal mountains. Within this band is the entire natural distribution of the Coast Redwood. It is perhaps the nation's most revered tree, the tree with a national park all its own.

To the east, away from the coast, the view from Cone Peak is wide and uninterrupted. In winter and spring when the air is clean and sharp, it's possible to look two hundred miles straight across the state and into the mouth of Yosemite Valley. Here too is another of California's well-known endemics, a near relative of the Coast Redwood: the Big Tree or Giant Sequoia. The range for these trees is even more restricted. All native members of the species grow in about 75 groves centered in the lower Sierra Nevada, ending in an isolated stand of a few trees due west of Lake Tahoe.

The Giant Sequoia, Coast Redwood, and Santa Lucia Fir are perhaps the most famous of California's endemic plant species. Fossil needles and cones found widely in North America and Asia tell us that these trees are relict species, left behind in favorable locales after ancestral ranges had shrunk with changing climate and topography.

California, despite the length of its coastline, doesn't have many islands—maybe just over a dozen. But among them all, Santa Cruz Island stands out. From the shore near Santa Barbara, the island juts up as a tantalizing shape on the horizon, in clear weather its steep coastal ridges standing out as pleats in an otherwise featureless profile. From high above, as shown in satellite photos and maps, the island has the outline of a turkey dashing for its life—blunt tail in the west, plump body, and stretched-out neck, cockscomb, wattle, and beak in the east. At 96 square miles, Santa Cruz Island is quite large enough to get lost on. The topography is highly varied: a major fault cleaves the island through its core, and on either side of this big central valley are two distinct ranges of hills (they've even been called mountains), one rising to 2,400 feet.

Cutting down through these hills are scores of winding canyons, some alive year-round with the sound of running water, others silent. And growing up through the canyons are thickets of Coastal Sage, Coyote Brush, Deer Brush, and willow, all surrounded by broad, open grasslands. At intervals, groves of round-crowned oaks and lanky pines stand out from the chaparral. It's along these margins that a visitor is likely to hear the rasping screech of the Santa Cruz Island Scrub Jay.

The usual Scrub Jay, which inhabits western woodlands and chaparral margins, looks a bit like a cross between an eastern Blue Jay and a very small crow: although it has no crest, it has the jay's characteristic stout, powerful bill, and the head, wings, and tail are a deep iridescent blue. On Santa Cruz Island the Scrub Jay is different. The subspecies endemic to the island is significantly larger and bluer than its mainland counterpart, with a recognizably larger beak.

One of the Scrub Jay's roles, for whatever reason, is to comment loudly on the passage of other animals through its habitat. On Santa Cruz the jay is often heard shrieking after a diminutive gray-and-tan fox. The fox, too, is highly unusual. Gray Foxes are common in wild California—that is, on the mainland. Offshore, six of California's eight Channel Islands harbor a related but distinct species, the Island Fox. And each of these islands supports a different subspecies.

Both the Santa Cruz Island Fox and Scrub Jay are excellent examples of endemism among California's animal populations. A great many others are found on California's islands as well as on the mainland: the Island Night Lizard, restricted to three other islands but mysteriously absent from Santa Cruz; the Yellow-billed Magpie, a California endemic found mainly in the Great Central Valley; the Salt Marsh Harvest Mouse, confined to dwindling tidelands around San Francisco Bay; the Blunt-nosed Leopard Lizard, now endangered after near-total agricultural conversions of its habitat in the southern San Joaquin

Valley; and the Red-bellied Newt, isolated in the state's North Coast region. The list goes on.

How do these animals fit into the whole California picture? The state supports roughly 965 native vertebrates: 540 birds, 77 reptiles, 47 amphibians, 214 mammals, 83 freshwater fishes, give or take a few in each category. Somewhere around 65 of these species live only in California. These are all full species, not subspecies. With subspecies you'd have a lot of local endemics—almost any isolated valley would have some endemic subspecies. How many statewide?

The numbers get squishy because not all species and subspecies are created equal. Scientific names reflect naturalists' attempts to document observed variation, but not all organisms have been treated similarly or studied in equal detail. Some classified as "full" distinct species are closely related and are known to have separated recently via minor genetic changes. On the other hand, some subspecies—like those of the California Slender Salamander—look nearly identical, yet at the molecular level are as different as robins and ostriches, a "genetic distance" that evolved over millions of years. Such a difference can be discerned only by biochemical analysis. Taxonomists are still struggling to work it all out.

For the rest of us forced to accept the taxonomy as it stands, California's biotic richness is simply there to see on any walk in the wilds. And this see-it-yourself natural diversity, not the polysyllabic names and the hyperbolic tallies, is what has conservationists and land managers concerned. Since the discovery of gold, California has been growing fiercely: In 1985 the state's population reached 25.6 million, surpassing that of New York, the next most populous state, by nearly eight million residents.

Fortunately, the land itself is large. California covers as much area as New York, Ohio, and all the New England states combined. Unfortunately, *wild* California is shrinking. Since 1900, to give just one example, at least sixty-five percent of the state's coastal wetlands have been dredged, filled, or drained. Eliminated with the life-giving mud were the resident shorebirds, crabs, clams, fishes, and mammals. It is difficult to say how much of the state can no longer support its original communities of plants and animals—perhaps twenty-five percent or more. What can be said is that development pressures remain severe. Urban sprawl, agricultural expansion, logging, mining, energy development, and road building have diminished every type of habitat.

Although not one of the state's natural communities has yet been wiped out, some are only the breadth of a bulldozer's blade away from extinction. The riparian forests of the Great Central Valley, once covering hundreds of square miles, are now nearly gone. Of a community called Southern Coastal Dune Scrub, only three hundred acres are left.

Vernal pools and their unusual plant assemblages are endangered statewide. For some natural elements, such as the Southern Coastal Dune Scrub, a single catastrophe could eliminate all the remaining habitat.

Things have clearly reached a critical stage for natural diversity in the Golden State. As Harvard biologist Edward O. Wilson warns, "The one process ongoing in the 1980s that will take millions of years to correct is the loss of genetic and species diversity by the destruction of natural habitats. This is the folly our descendants are least likely to forgive us."

If we don't speed up the preservation of natural habitats or face up to the bitter possibility that elements of the state's ecological matrix will soon be lost, wild California will dwindle piece by piece beyond recovery.

— *Sheridan Warrick*

A native Californian, Sheridan Warrick is formerly the editor of *Pacific Discovery*, the quarterly magazine of the California Academy of Sciences, and managing editor of the Academy's scholarly *Proceedings* and *Occasional Papers*. He is the author of several publications and popular articles on science and natural history.

California Nature Conservancy Preserves

1. *McCloud River,* Shasta County
2. *Lanphere-Christensen Dunes,* Humboldt County
3. *Northern California Coast Range,* Mendocino County
4. *Vina Plains,* Tehama County
5. *Boggs Lake,* Lake County
6. *Fairfield Osborn,* Sonoma County
7. *Ring Mountain,* Marin County
8. *Cosumnes River,* Sacramento County
9. *Jepson Prairie,* Solano County

10. *Elkhorn Slough,* Monterey County
11. *Landels-Hill Big Creek,* Monterey County
12. *Kaweah Oaks,* Tulare County
13. *Creighton Ranch,* Tulare County
14. *Pixley Vernal Pools,* Tulare County
15. *Paine Wildflower,* Kern County
16. *Kern River,* Kern County
17. *Carrizo Plain,* San Luis Obispo County

18. *Desert Tortoise,* Kern County
19. *Santa Cruz Island,* Santa Barbara County
20. *Big Bear Valley,* San Bernadino County
21. *Big Morongo,* San Bernadino County
22. *Coachella Valley,* Riverside County
23. *Santa Rosa Plateau,* Riverside County

Introduction

Well-kept Secrets

TWO HOURS' drive from downtown Los Angeles, Bald Eagles still soar over a lakefront that harbors more species of rare and endangered plants than any other single location in the country. Within view of San Francisco's skyscrapers, cinnamon-petaled lilies found nowhere else on earth find protection. Just a long tee shot from the fairways of Palm Springs, curious-looking lizards from the Pleistocene, now saved from extinction, sprint across dunes of blow-sand. And fewer than thirty miles south of Sacramento, Greater Sandhill Cranes find sanctuary alongside the only large free-flowing river left in the Great Central Valley.

These sites and sights are anomalies on the urban edge, yet they are living proof that you don't have to travel far to get a close-up and uncrowded look at California's ecologically diverse and rich natural world. They are part of a lightly visited system of nature preserves that protects rare and endangered wildlife in its natural habitat.

The network of preserves is the creation of The Nature Conservancy, a nonprofit, nonpartisan, national conservation organization dedicated solely to protecting natural beauty and biological diversity through habitat preservation. Using easements, donations, exchanges, and outright purchases, the Conservancy quietly and with little fanfare has acquired some 4,700 parcels of ecologically important land scattered throughout the United States, the Caribbean, and Latin America. The Conservancy currently manages about a thousand of these areas as natural preserves.

The California preserves range in size from a tiny patch of the San Joaquin Valley to a vast tract of desolate desert wilderness — to as much as ninety percent of the largest island off the Southern California coast. Each preserve is biologically unique and irreplaceable, and many support the last habitats of their kind left in the world. Collectively, they preserve representational habitats from all of the state's biological provinces. The Nature Conservancy is the only organization that manages such a network. Not even the state park system represents such a cross section. Though privately owned, these preserves are open to the public free of charge.

These preserves reflect the state's incredible variety of ecosystems and the wide array of wildlife species they support. No other state comes close to matching California's natural diversity. From high and low deserts to northern rain forests, from subtropical scrublands to pine and oak woodlands, from great marshy deltas to subalpine forests and alpine meadows, California has it all.

But California also has the country's biggest population. Almost a million people move to the Golden State each year. By the year 2000, the census will record 33 million. The population explosion and attendant agricultural, urban, and industrial boom have already consumed huge portions of those precious and irreplaceable lands that made California an ecological cornucopia in the first place. Further growth threatens to devour much of what remains. In many cases, the only thing standing between some of the state's most delicate ecosystems and total destruction is a Nature Conservancy preserve.

Loss of habitat translates directly into loss of life — wildlife. The enormity of the situation is staggering. Many historic occurrences of thousands of California species and natural communities have completely vanished. At least fifty known species are presumed extinct in the state, including the California Grizzly Bear, Cascades Gray Wolf, Long-eared Kit Fox, Santa Barbara Song Sparrow, San Clemente Bewick's Wren, Xerces Blue Butterfly, Los Angeles Sunflower, Mendocino Bush Mallow, and Showy Indian Clover.

Sadly, the list is sure to grow as the trend continues. More than 800 species of animals and plants could follow the grizzly and wolf into oblivion during the next generation. One-third of California's animal species, nearly a quarter of its birds, and over half of the state's 5,000 native plant species are at risk. Already the U.S. Fish and Wildlife Service and the California Department of Fish and Game have designated 270 California species as endangered, threatened, or rare. Hundreds more are candidates for listing. By definition, an endangered species is one in danger of extinction throughout all or a significant portion of its range, and a threatened species is one likely to become so within the foreseeable future.

Extinction. Nothing is as final, as irreversible, as unconscionable. Cliched as it sounds, extinction is forever. The extirpation of a species or natural community is one of the few consequences of human activity that is truly irreparable.

Yet, despite the state's plethora of diverse habitats and niches, California's wildlife is edging closer to the brink of mass extinction. At risk is our biodiversity, the genetic pool that ensures a healthy, balanced ecosystem. Habitat destruction threatens to desolate the land with a virulence biologists compare to limited nuclear war. The fallout from the loss of genetic and species diversity will take millions of years to repair.

The social, economic, medical, and genetic benefits to saving natural habitats are readily apparent. Biodiversity is the foundation of life. We depend on a large and diverse gene pool for many of the plants and animals that provide us with such useful materials as lumber, fuel, food, medicines, and industrial chemicals. Bacteria and plants, for instance, supply us with chemicals for over one-half of all prescriptions written annually in the United States. Antiviral agents and arthritis and high blood pressure medications are just a few examples. Regular infusions of fresh genetic material from wild plants are also used to maintain many of our major food crops, including corn, wheat, barley, tomatoes, and oranges. New ways of using them are constantly being discovered: A rare species of wild corn recently identified in Mexico may be crossbred with conventional strains of corn to produce a hybrid immune to four diseases; U.S. wheat growers are benefiting from a wild strain of wheat introduced from Turkey. The list goes on.

No doubt other plants harbor equally useful compounds and genetic stock, but, unfortunately, there is no thorough inventory of life on earth. Many of the species threatened with mass extinction remain unknown to us. Unless steps are taken, we will lose their potential benefit forever.

The Nature Conservancy was one of the first groups to recognize this problem, and it has been working to prevent the loss of biodiversity for more than eighty years. Born out of two committees formed by the Ecological Society of America in 1917, the Arlington, Virginia-based organization has grown to become the largest private owner of land sanctuaries in the world. To date, the Conservancy has preserved a collection of real estate about the size of Delaware and Rhode Island combined — more than three million acres that are home to over a thousand different species of rare plants and animals.

The Conservancy made its first California acquisition in 1958 when a small band of dedicated volunteers successfully concluded protracted negotiations to purchase 4,000 acres of old-growth Douglas-fir forest and an undisturbed tributary of the Eel River. The site became known as the Northern California Coast Range Preserve. Within its thickly wooded boundaries dwell a number of imperiled species, including the elusive Spotted Owl.

With that success, volunteer land acquisition activity quickly expanded in the state, helped in part by increasing efforts from a fledgling professional staff at the Conservancy's Western Regional Office in San Francisco. The result was a growing list of preserves, among them the second largest estuary in the state, Elkhorn Slough near Monterey, and six pristine miles of the McCloud River at the base of Mount Shasta.

Confidence grew with each achievement, and by 1977 the Conservancy took on a near-impossible task for those times—the $1.8 million acquisition of 3,800 acres of redwood forest and 22 other distinct plant communities on California's spectacular Big Sur coast. In less than a year, the Conservancy, working with the University of California, completed the fund-raising campaign and created the Landels-Hill Big Creek Preserve.

By then the escalating number and size of projects required the full-time attention of a professional staff. The California Field Office was formed in 1977. Its first project, as ambitious as it was bold, was the preservation of ninety percent of 62,000-acre Santa Cruz Island. Undaunted by the scope of the challenge, the Conservancy plunged ahead, and within two years succeeded in raising the $4 million necessary to secure the future of this unique sanctuary in the sea.

To ensure that its land protection efforts concentrated on sites of highest biological significance, the Conservancy worked with the state's Department of Fish and Game to create the California Natural Diversity Data Base, a computerized inventory of rare and threatened species and natural communities. The data base, operated by the department's California Natural Heritage Section in Sacramento, holds more than 16,000 up-to-date locational records on over 1,200 species and biotic communities.

Using preliminary information gathered by the data base, the Conservancy launched the California Critical Areas Program, a three-year, $15.5-million plan to safeguard the state's most endangered biological communities. By the end of 1983, the California Nature Conservancy had established eleven new preserves totaling some 16,000 acres—critical habitat for over fifty rare species or natural ecosystems. The new preserves included a mountain in Tiburon where several rare plant species grow, a stand of highly endangered Valley Oaks outside of Visalia, a desert oasis where over 270 different species of birds congregate, and a former Spanish land grant midway between Los Angeles and San Diego that is a rich mosaic of Engelmann Oak woodland and savanna, vernal pools, and expanses of native bunchgrass.

Bolstered by the success of the Critical Areas Program, and guided by the extensive findings of the Natural Diversity Data Base, the California Nature Conservancy initiated its most comprehensive and ambitious statewide effort to date: the Wild California campaign. The objectives of this four-year, $20-million preservation program are to preserve the state's species and natural communities most in jeopardy, to research why species are in decline, and to restore habitats in conservation ownership. In addition, the program is establishing permanent mechanisms that will provide the best means of safeguarding other imperiled biological features as they are identified. A significant aspect is the extensive cooperation and coordination with public agencies and other private organizations, which is greatly expanding the Conservancy's efficacy. Sites are being protected using the most appropriate of three approaches: outright acquisition, public agency collaboration, and landowner notification.

Cooperation, not confrontation, has always been The Nature Conservancy's *modus operandi*. It takes no political positions, backs no candidates, and avoids controversy. Working positively to get beneficial projects accomplished has enabled the Conservancy to undertake numerous multimillion dollar projects, thanks to the generosity of individuals, foundations, and corporations. Private enterprise identifies with The Nature Conservancy's objectives, because the organization operates like a business itself. Leveraged capital, management agreements, bargain purchases, low-interest loans, conservation easements, land exchanges, public/private partnerships, and outright purchase—these are the methods it uses.

Acquiring land is only half the job, however. The Nature Conservancy also plays an active role in managing it. Staff ecologists conduct exhaustive site investigations to identify a preserve's natural elements, the species and communities that populate the land. Management plans are designed and implemented to help protect and, in some cases, restore a site to its original condition. At tiny Pixley Vernal Pools Preserve in the Central Valley, for instance, controlled burning is used to help encourage the growth of native plants and retard alien species. At Kern River Preserve, east of Bakersfield, hundreds of acres of cottonwoods and willows have been planted to replace lost riparian habitat vital to the recovery of the endangered Yellow-billed Cuckoo.

The Conservancy relies heavily on its active membership to help maintain its network of preserves. More than 60,000 Californians are members. Several of the preserves have full-time, resident staff managers, but most are cared for by volunteers under the direction of a professional staff. Everything from interpretive walks for visitors to field surveys of rare elements are organized, and members help clear trails, build fences, and count birds.

To most appreciate The Nature Conservancy's work, you have to experience it firsthand. You have to see a shiny, red-striped Shasta Rainbow Trout leaping out of the turquoise waters of the McCloud River in pursuit of a stonefly, watch a Desert Bighorn Sheep nimbly work its way down a rocky slope at Big Morongo Canyon in search of water, catch the sunset at Creighton Ranch as thousands of ducks and geese silhouetted against the sky prepare to land on the freshwater marsh, marvel at the concentric bands of colorful wildflowers that encircle the vernal pools at Jepson Prairie, and witness the age-old battle between shifting sand and primeval forest at Lanphere-Christensen Dunes. These irreplaceable natural treasures are among the most well-kept secrets in the state.

The Conservancy's lands are open to the public and visitation is encouraged. But inherent in the maintenance of healthy ecosystems is the understanding that the visitor, whether seeking solitude, recreation, or scientific knowledge, is a transient guest in the living quarters of sensitive plants and animals. Respect and care are due the residents. If the survival of these species is to be ensured, their needs must supersede all other activities. Understandably, some restrictions do apply. Regulations governing use vary from preserve to preserve, but, generally, vehicles, pets, firearms, smoking, hunting, camping, collecting, and littering are not allowed. In addition, park only in designated areas, leave gates the way you found them, use stiles to protect fencing from excessive wear, and stick to the trails.

The Conservancy keeps facilities and trail development to a minimum; old structures and paths are often removed or closed off. Trails that are created and maintained are designed to give visitors a good look at the preserve while safeguarding its natural qualities. Because the Conservancy's philosophy regarding use of its preserves is a cautious one—and because most of the areas lack visitor facilities—it's always a good idea to contact the preserve office before arriving. That way you can receive up-to-date information on special use restrictions as well as schedules for guided tours.

Many preserves are open to the public only through guided tours. Some are open every day on a drop-in basis. They also feature guided tours, but offer in addition the opportunity for individuals and small groups to explore these unique areas.

This book introduces twenty-three of The Nature Conservancy's most accessible and representative California preserves. Each preserve description is followed by a map and handy checklist with detailed information for arranging a visit. The guide is intended to provide an overview of a preserve's natural history and an appreciation of what makes it unique. For convenience, common names for species are used throughout the text, and an appendix cross-referencing them with their scientific names has been included.

If you plan to visit on your own, remember you will be seeing many species and habitats that are not ordinarily viewed by casual outdoor enthusiasts or even by professional naturalists. You will rarely encounter other guests. For some, this solitude is the ultimate prize; for others, joining a group visit to explore with a knowledgeable companion is a great reward.

When you visit a preserve, remember to bring field guides, binoculars, and a magnifying glass. The plants and animals don't have labels. Most of all, plan to explore slowly. After all, when it came time to create California's wild lands, nature wasn't in a rush.

NORTH

ONE

McCloud River

Land of Rainbows

WHEN THE first thermals of summer blow gentle, billowy gasps of warm air into Northern California's river canyons, that's the signal to hang up the proverbial Gone Fishin' sign and head for the solace and solitude of the hills. Incubating insects spring to life, dancing across the waters in clouds as they hatch. Trout awaken from their winter torpor, driven to fits of feeding frenzy.

The Golden Stonefly hatch on the McCloud River is one of the more remarkable of these entomophagous extravaganzas. Remarkable also is the piscine participant, the Shasta Rainbow, highly prized because the strain is pure and not yet diluted by hatchery-bred trout. What makes a fishing pilgrimage to the McCloud even more rewarding is that no more than nine other anglers are found at a time on the best part of the river, two and one-half pristine miles managed by The Nature Conservancy.

The McCloud River starts out as meltwater trickling into porous rock on the glacier-crusted slopes of 14,000-foot Mount Shasta. This cold, pure water eventually makes its way to the base of the mountain where it bursts forth from the canyon wall at Big Springs, 44 degrees and gin clear, to form the headwaters. The river then makes a headlong descent to the south, slashing through a thick forest of Douglas-fir at a drop rate of fifty feet per mile. Mud Creek, entering the McCloud farther downstream, tints the river turquoise-gray from ash and glacial silt. Uplifted metamorphic rock creates perfect habitat for trout—stretches of riffles and rapids, and deep pools hemmed in by huge boulders.

The river has cut a steep, narrow canyon that teems with wildlife. Two species, the Shasta Salamander and a plant named Shasta Eupatory, flourish on limestone outcrops in this area and occur nowhere else on earth. Mountain Lion, Black Bear, Ringtail, River Otter, Mink, Bald Eagle, and Spotted Owl also call the McCloud home.

The Wintu Indians relied on the river's resources for centuries. They lived in shallow pit houses on its banks, spearing and trapping salmon and steelhead as the fish made seasonal journeys to and from the sea. In 1829, a Hudson's Bay Company trapper, Alexander McLeod, was the first white man to discover the river. It is named (albeit misspelled) after him.

The Railroad Act of 1862 handed the river and surrounding lands over to the Central Pacific Railroad Company. Tracks were never laid, but the McCloud soon gained a reputation for its prolific fishery. In 1872, an egg-taking station was installed at the mouth of the river, and Shasta Rainbows, known for their brilliant colors and strong fight when caught, were exported all over the world.

The river's popularity grew as well. By the 1920s, most of the river corridor had been purchased by private fishing clubs and individuals, including publishing czar William Randolph Hearst. He purchased 60,000 acres along seven miles of the upper river, built a number of "castles" along its thickly wooded banks, and called the family summer retreat Wyntoon.

The river remained relatively unmolested until the completion of Shasta Dam in 1945. The enormous impoundment just to the south of the McCloud's confluence with the Sacramento completely blocked the huge salmon and steelhead runs and flooded fifteen miles of the lower river canyon forever. Twenty years later, another smaller dam was constructed on the McCloud's upper section, creating a six-mile reservoir there.

Sandwiched between these two dams, the middle of the river has survived, thanks in part to the generosity of the McCloud River Club, one of the oldest private fishing clubs in California. Members donated six miles of their holdings to The Nature Conservancy in 1973, out of concern for the river's safety. Initially, the Conservancy's objective was to protect the native fishery. An extensive biological inventory was conducted in 1974 and 1975, and the research indicated that a portion of the preserve could be opened to carefully managed public use, including catch-and-release fishing. In recognition of the endeavor, the California Fish and Game Commission designated a section of the river, which included the preserve, as an official Wild Trout Stream in 1975. The following year the McCloud River Preserve welcomed visitors for the first time.

Two and one-half miles of the river are open to the public. The rest is managed solely for wildlife and scientific research. Protective measures have been designed to ensure the unique character of the river and its dependent wildlife. No roads go through the preserve, just a footpath. Only ten fishermen are allowed on the river at any one time; five spots are available by reservation, five on a drop-in basis. Anglers may use spinning or fly equipment here, but the creel limit is zero; fishing is

◄ *McCloud River Preserve*

catch-and-release only. Single, barbless hooks are required to make release easy.

Shasta Rainbow aren't the only fish harbored by the preserve. The only California river that could do so, the McCloud until recently supported Dolly Varden Char, a northern coldwater member of the salmon family related to Eastern Brook Trout and Lake Trout. This dark-green fish with red and yellow spots was perhaps named after the Charles Dickens' character who wore a flower-trimmed hat and red polka-dot print dress in his novel *Barnaby Rudge.*

The species was probably widely distributed during the Ice Age, but warming and drying of the climate during the last 10,000 years reduced its range. Evidently, the cold, fast-moving stable flows of the McCloud had become its southernmost refuge. Unfortunately, the number of Dolly Varden has dropped dramatically, possibly to the point of extinction, since the completion of the Shasta and McCloud dams.

For the past several years the Conservancy and the Department of Fish and Game have been conducting an extensive investigation into the fish's demise. Fishermen at the preserve have been encouraged to help in the study. Every pool has a five-gallon plastic bucket with instructions for anglers to transport suspected Dolly Varden to nearby live cages and to alert the preserve staff. A fish weir, which is basically a fence across the river with built-in live traps, has also been used to search for Dollies, but none have been found for many years. The California Department of Fish and Game is now considering reintroduction of Dolly Varden Char in the McCloud.

Another fish found in the McCloud is the Brown Trout. It was first introduced to the river by sportsmen in the mid-1920s. Its numbers have increased significantly since the dam was completed. Scientists now suspect the voracious trout has displaced the Dolly Varden by filling the degraded niche of the vanishing char. Brown Trout tagged in the river average 19 to 23 inches; the record is a female that measured 39 inches and weighed 13 pounds.

The chance to test your piscatory proficiency isn't the only reason to visit the McCloud River Preserve. An opportunity to explore a river canyon where the timeless continuum of life remains relatively unbroken by modern man is reason enough.

A walk along the preserve's interpretive trail reveals a mixed forest filled with botanical delights. The path is shaded by several species of cone-bearing trees; the most common is Douglas-fir, followed by Ponderosa and Sugar pines, and Incense Cedar. Surprisingly, White Fir also grows here despite the 2,000-foot elevation. This species is normally found at higher altitudes, but the preserve's rugged topography has created a unique microclimate that closely resembles the high country. Another evergreen, the Western Yew, is also present. Its bark is like manzanita and the foliage is delicate and a brighter green than that of fir. The Wintu used its wood for bows. In fact, its scientific name, *Taxus*, is a classical Latin word derived from the Greek word for bow, "taxon." Species of oak that flourish in the canyon are California Black Oak, Canyon Live Oak, and Oregon Oak.

Beneath the forest canopy is a tangled understory of Snowberry, Deer Brush, Poison-oak, Squaw Bush, Big-leaf Maple, and Pacific Dogwood. Greenbrier, a relative to the plant used to make the old-time drink sarsaparilla, entwines the trunks of Western Plum. On the hot, dry slopes, Redbud grows in clumps. Its lavender-red flowers cover the bare branches in April and May before the shrubs leaf out. A mat of Wintergreen, Star Flower, Wild Rose, Fairy Bells, lupine, violets, and Douglas's Iris covers the ground.

Small animals scuffle for food in the dry leaves. Songbirds call, and Steller's Jays scold in the trees above. Western Gray Squirrels transport acorns for winter storage, inadvertently playing tree planter when forgotten buried caches sprout and grow the following spring.

Old-growth forest of Douglas-fir and Ponderosa Pine grace areas of the canyon slopes. Such sensitive species as the Wolverine persist here, sharing the forest with Mountain Lion and Spotted Owl. Tributary streams tumble down the steep canyon walls in cataracts to join the McCloud.

At streamside the vegetation is dominated by White Alder and shocks of Indian Rhubarb, whose prehistoric-looking leaves droop in the current. Stalks of horsetail, a plant whose history dates back 300 million years, rise at water's edge.

Life is active along the river. Mink cavort over slick rocks as River Otters glide across large pools in search of trout. Dippers bob on fallen trees, Bald Eagles soar overhead. And Black Bears use the riverbank trails as highways, so don't be surprised if you have an audience while fishing.

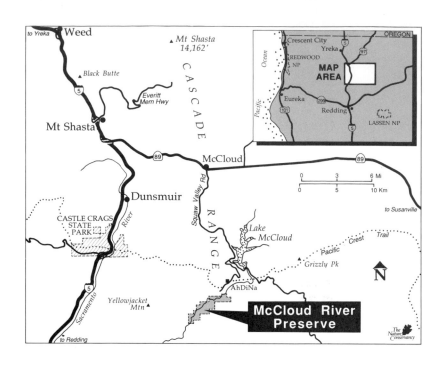

McCloud River Checklist

INFORMATION

McCloud River Preserve opens at sunrise and closes at sunset. No more than 10 anglers are allowed on the preserve at any one time. Five places may be reserved through the Conservancy's Field Office in San Francisco, 785 Market St., 3rd Floor, 94103; (415) 777-0487. The remainder are available on a first-come, first-served basis. There is a self-guided nature trail. For more information, contact the preserve manager at P.O. Box 409, McCloud, CA 96057; (916) 926-4366.

SIZE

2,330 acres

SEASONAL HIGHLIGHTS

Spring is alive with flowers and wildlife; trout fishing is best spring through fall; and in fall, foliage is brilliantly colored.

WEATHER

Mediterranean climate. Autumn brings Indian summer weather, winter is snowbound, and summer is hot.

ON-SITE FACILITIES

Preserve headquarters, self-guided nature trail, information kiosk, and five miles of hiking trails.

NEAREST OFF-SITE FACILITIES

One hour's drive over dirt road to town of McCloud. Overnight camping available 1½ miles upstream at low-cost USFS campground.

EQUIPMENT

fishing equipment
camping equipment
good walking shoes
binoculars
food and water
mosquito repellent

TIME REQUIRED

All day minimum

DIRECTIONS

McCloud River is about a six-hour drive from San Francisco. To get there, take Interstate 5 north to State Highway 89. Head east to the town of McCloud. Turn right at the Shell station and follow the signs to Ah-Di-Na campground. Ten miles of the access road are unpaved, narrow in spots, winding, and may have sharp or large rocks. But the road is not steep or slippery. One mile past the campground, the road dead-ends at the preserve trailhead. Park here and follow the trail one-half mile to the preserve headquarters.

Lanphere-Christensen Dunes

Where Sand and Forest Collide

THOUGH MOST of California's fragile coastal dunes have disappeared beneath housing tracts and dune buggy tracks, a thriving remnant holds fast on a narrow sand spit stretching between the mouth of the Mad River and Humboldt Bay on the very edge of California's rain-soaked North Coast.

Here on 338 acres, shifting sands engage the forest in mortal combat for territory. Ceaseless winds weave beautiful and complex patterns across towering dunes eighty feet high. In summertime, tenacious wild-flowers turn lunar landscapes into seas of color.

At this latitude, southern and northern dune floras overlap, making this dune system unique to the West Coast. Blooming in large, defiant clumps are evening primroses, morning glories, Seaside Daisies, and a relatively abundant population of Menzies' Wallflower, a rare and endangered member of the Mustard family. This fragile plant grows in only six other locations in the state. The preserve is also home to two endemic plants, Humboldt Bay Owl's Clover and Humboldt Bay Gum Plant.

Along the edge of dunes a unique biotic web stretches between stands of Sitka Spruce and Beach Pine. A relative of the slender Lodgepole Pine, the Beach Pine's stunted growth attests to the habitat's demanding conditions. The forest supports an extremely diverse faunal community. Over two hundred species of birds have been identified at the preserve, including the curious-looking Red Crossbill. Males in their brick-red plumes cling to pine cones, noisily extracting seeds with their peculiar bills. Snowy Owls from the Arctic have touched down in winter months on their annual migration south.

A thousand years ago, Wiyot Indians camped on the dunes and lived off fish and clams they took from the ocean and mudflats and rabbits and quail they hunted in the forests. The wind occasionally uncovers one of their ancient shell middens. Some of these long-forgotten mounds

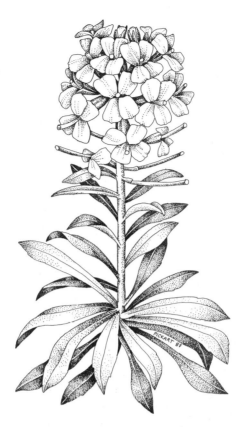

Menzies' Wallflower

contain stone sinkers used for fishing nets, spear and arrow points, and knives and drills.

Later, white settlers diked and drained the nearby salt marshes and used the land for grazing cattle. In the early 1940s, William and Hortense Lanphere, both biologists at Humboldt State University in nearby Arcata, purchased a significant portion of the area. They immediately recognized the intrinsic value of the land, and, together with their neighbor, I. Darrel Christensen, decided to protect its natural history. They fenced and posted the dunes and patrolled them to keep out off-road vehicles. It's said that Mrs. Lanphere used to chase off trespassers with a rifle.

In 1974, the Lanpheres deeded a conservation easement and Christensen sold his acreage to the California Nature Conservancy, so the special place could be forever preserved. An adjoining 30 acres to the north were purchased in 1981 from the Hunt family. Five years later, 130 acres bordering the preserve to the south were acquired from the Hutton family. The Lanpheres donated the fee title to their property the same year.

The preserve is cooperatively managed by the Conservancy and a committee comprising Humboldt State University faculty members. It is used by students and professors alike for scientific research and education.

The sanctuary supports one of the two remaining examples of Northern Foredune Grassland communities in the state, as well as Northern Foredune, Northern Coastal Salt Marsh, and Beach Pine Forest.

Very few places exist where the rugged northern Pacific shoreline becomes flat and wide enough for the formation of sand dunes, but at Lanphere-Christensen, conditions are just right. Each stage of dune evolution is illustrated here in striking clarity, from the first build-up of shifting sand to the climax Sitka Spruce forest.

A remarkably dynamic ecosystem, the beach/dunes/forest complex is created by the interaction between river-supplied sand, the prevailing northwest winds, and the colonizing and stabilizing efforts of plant species. The barrier spit derives its sand principally from the Mad River, which in the geologic past emptied into ancestral Humboldt Bay. Winds blow the sand to the foredune, where it is trapped by stabilizing native grasses. Behind the foredune is found a series of hollows, or a deflation plain, formed by the erosive action of the wind. Erosion in the hollows is slowed only when the capillary fringe of the local water table is reached. At that time plant colonization occurs in the resulting wet depressions.

The same process helps vegetate the ridges between the large sand waves. Plants colonize the slower moving flanks of the large sand dunes, sending long roots, or rhizomes, through the sand in all directions to help stabilize the dunes even further. In the more rapidly moving centers of these sand waves, sand is blown farther downwind, eventually leaving a hollow flanked by a pair of vegetated ridges. Much of the present forest area consists of such an alternating series of old lateral dune ridges separated by a parallel series of hollows.

Each of the zones is characterized by a distinctive native plant community. The upper strand and foredunes support a native Dune Grass that is hard to find in other parts of the state. It has been largely crowded out by imported European Beach Grass. Dune ridges behind the primary foredune are covered with a diverse community of forbs and subshrubs whose flowers account for much of the summer color on the dunes. Bush Lupine, another exotic, threatens this Northern Foredune community.

Sedges, rushes, and willows invade the lower wet hollows behind the foredunes. Beach Pine dominates the distinctive, vegetated ridges between the large dunes, and the forest areas are covered by a mixed community of Beach Pine and Sitka Spruce that shades an understory of California Huckleberry and other shrubs.

The dunes both protect and battle the forest, each retreating where the other advances, renegotiating their boundaries constantly. The forest forms in older hollows or advances out on the interdune ridges. Higher dunes actually provide a shield against the sandy, salt-burning winds, thus protecting the forest.

Dunes play an important practical function in the transition zone between land and sea. Like coastal marshes, they stabilize the coastline and prevent the loss of land. Unfortunately, their natural features are fragile, their existence tenuous. Human impact can be disastrous. Even too much walking on a dune can destroy the cover of vegetation, leaving it open to more than usual erosion. This vulnerability to trampling is so well understood in land-scarce Holland, for instance, that access to grass-covered dunes is denied to the public.

Take care, then, when you follow the well-marked trail that leads from the entrance of the preserve. It takes you through a tunnel in the trees and out onto a drift of sand bleached white as bone and ribbed by furrows carved by wind. You'll notice native grasses that run along the tops of the dunes and patches of Beach Pea, Coast Buckwheat, and Sand-verbena struggling against the constantly moving sand.

The trail goes down to the ocean, follows along a spit of driftwood-studded sand that points to the mouth of Humboldt Bay, then leads back across the dunes and into the forest again. Along the battle line between sand and tree, skeletons of treetops smothered by the never-ending wave raise their limbs in mute surrender.

Where trees have survived, however, vegetation reigns supreme. The forest floor is blanketed by miniature manzanita known as Bearberry and Reindeer Lichen—two species of the Arctic tundra that migrated south in earlier times of climatic cooling and survived subsequent warming trends in this moderate marine environment. The lichen is as white as snow and grows in dense, spongy patches in winter. It dies in summer. Interwoven with Bearberry, Beach Pine seedlings, Salal, and ferns, it makes for a colorful and strikingly beautiful groundcover. The preserve also hosts other species of lichen as well. In fact, approximately fifteen distributions of lichen species new to the state and two species new to North America have been identified.

The forest itself is a veritable greenhouse for plants. Several types of orchids thrive, including Ladies' Tresses, Calypsos, Rein Orchids, and Rattlesnake-plantains. More than two hundred species of fungi are also to be found. Biologists have discovered at least 23 types either new to science, new to California, or new to North America. In the fall, millions of mushrooms splashed red, yellow, purple, and lavender transform the forest into a mycologist's paradise.

All the flora helps sustain a healthy population of fauna. Gray Foxes make dens in the dense cover of huckleberry and willows. Striped

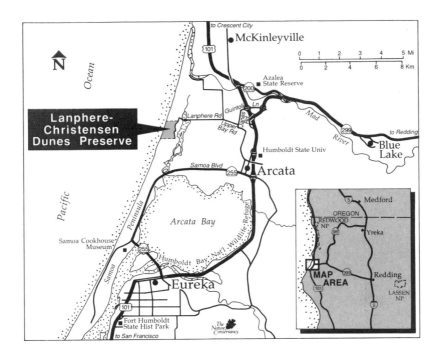

Skunks, Porcupines, Raccoons, Bobcats, and Long-tailed Weasels are also present. The Grand Fir and Sitka Spruce trees serve as perches for fifteen species of raptors, including owls and falcons. At dusk, herons and egrets return from a day's hunting in the salt marshes to roost in the tallest spruces. The denseness of the forest hides many of the birds from view, but you can certainly hear them. Their squawks, screeches, hoots, and shrieks pierce the canopy of moss-laden trees, adding an air of mystery to the primeval place.

◄ *Lanphere-Christensen Dunes Preserve*

Lanphere-Christensen Dunes Checklist

INFORMATION

Guided tours are held every Saturday at 10 A.M. from September through June, departing from parking lot. Other use is by permission only. Call in advance for permit. The public must first attend a Saturday walk to become acquainted with trails and use policies. For a permit, brochure or information, contact the preserve's office at 6800 Lanphere Rd., Arcata, CA 95521; (707) 822-6378.

SIZE

338 acres

SEASONAL HIGHLIGHTS

Every month is special; June brings peak bloom of dune wild-flowers and late fall offers colorful fungi.

WEATHER

In spring and summer expect morning fog and afternoon wind. Rain is common in winter.

ON-SITE FACILITIES

Trails

NEAREST OFF-SITE FACILITIES

5 miles east in Arcata

EQUIPMENT

raingear (for October through April)
mosquito repellent (for forest walks April through September)
soft-soled walking shoes
binoculars
food and water

TIME REQUIRED

3 to 4 hours

DIRECTIONS

Lanphere-Christensen is six hours north of San Francisco via Highway 101. Take Giuntoli Lane exit off 101 north of Arcata, turn left. You'll be on Janes Road, which will swing to the south. After Mad River Hospital (on right) turn left onto Upper Bay Road and follow it to the end (it will turn into Lanphere Road). At signed gate, turn left and proceed one-half mile to parking lot.

THREE

Northern California Coast Range Preserve

New Life for Old Growth

J UST FIFTY years ago California was covered by two to three million acres of centuries-old Douglas-firs, but then, as the need for lumber increased, the old trees began to fall. Today, less than three percent of the state's original old growth forest remains.

Fortunately, one of the largest remnants has been protected on the banks of the South Fork of the Eel River, 150 miles north of San Francisco. Here, on 7,520 acres, Douglas-firs and Coast Redwoods rise above a mixed understory of evergreens, hardwoods, and shrubs that survives in the filtered sunlight.

Old-growth forest supports a unique community of animals that have specially adapted to this dank, dark, verdant world. Some of the more unusual residents you'll find at the Northern California Coast Range Preserve are the rare Spotted Owl, the wary Ringtail, and the Red Tree Vole, a small tree-dwelling rodent that spends its entire life a hundred feet off the ground.

Established in 1959, the preserve is The Nature Conservancy's oldest acquisition in the western United States. Not surprisingly, it holds a special place in the hearts of many longtime California residents. And not just for sentimental reasons, either. Besides being breathtakingly beautiful, the preserve is rich in natural and cultural history, offers miles of hiking trails, and provides an unlimited source of research material for students and scientists.

The site's earliest human inhabitants were Kato Indians, the southernmost group of Athapascan-speaking people in northern California. The Indians collected Tanbark Oak acorns, which they ground into meal, and caught salmon and steelhead during the spawning season.

Homesteaders arrived in the late 1800s. They settled primarily alongside the eight meadows in the valley and built houses, planted fruit

Coast Redwood

trees, and raised livestock. The original pioneer families lent their names
to some of the preserve's most prominent features, such as Elder Creek
and Walker Meadow. As the Indians had done before them, the early
settlers relied on the land's natural resources for survival.

Trees provided a livelihood. The bark of the Tanbark Oak is rich in
tannic acid. Homesteaders collected and sold the bark to commercial
tanners who used it for processing leather.

Some of the larger redwoods and Douglas-firs were also harvested for
lumber. The giants were toppled by ax and crosscut saw. You can still
see the notches the pioneers cut in the sides of redwood stumps to hold
springboards in place. Notches gave the logger a place to stand during
the several days it took to fell a single tree. Shakes, rails, fenceposts, and
planks were used as building materials for homesteads. The leftovers
were loaded up and hauled to town for ready cash.

A public inn was built around the turn of the century. During its hey-
day, Wilderness Lodge was a popular destination for urban-weary San
Franciscans in search of rustic peace and quiet. The resort was hard hit
by the Depression, however, and closed soon after. In 1937, it was
destroyed by fire. A couple of the buildings that escaped the inferno are
now used to house groups visiting the preserve.

Commercial logging intensified in the decades that followed. The
threat to the forest so alarmed one area family — Heath and Marjorie
Angelo — that they began buying as much land as they could in order to

protect it. Eventually, the Angelos sold their holdings to The Nature Conservancy. The federal Bureau of Land Management designated its adjacent holdings as an Area of Critical Environmental Concern and has tirelessly protected the area for its ecological qualities.

The sprawling preserve is bisected by a dirt road that parallels the South Fork of the Eel River and provides easy access to the site's many splendors. Trails of varying length loop off it. Most follow the numerous creeks that feed into the Eel: Sugar, Skunk, Elder, and Fox. Each is worth the hike.

A visit to the preserve will bring you face to face with one of the most complex natural communities found in the state. Contained within its boundaries is an intricate mosaic of vegetation types dominated by Douglas-fir. The most important timber species in North America, the Douglas-fir is moderately shade-tolerant, and prefers cool, moist slopes with northern exposure. Seedlings often become established in the shade of another forest or vegetation type. The young trees grow slowly in the shade, but once a tree-fall opens the canopy to full sunlight, they rocket upwards, rapidly reaching 150 to 200 feet tall.

Douglas-fir are long-lived. They reach maturity in about 100 to 150 years, but can live to be 800 and a maximum of 1,200 years old. At that age, the forest acquires a unique composition and structure. Huge fallen logs clutter the ground, majestic old snags stand interspersed with live trees of varying age, and the multilayered canopy creates a cool, moist microclimate at the forest floor where sunlight rarely reaches.

The dead snags are an integral part of the forest ecosystem. Rotting cores of the old trees provide homes for a variety of wildlife, including Pileated Woodpeckers, Screech Owls, and Pacific Giant Salamanders. As the old trees decay, nutrients in their wood return to the soil. The same is true for the dead logs that lie scattered across the forest floor like a giant's game of pick-up-sticks. Each rotting log is literally crawling with life — a small ecosystem in itself. Mushrooms or fungi attach themselves, a signal of the decaying process common to all living things. The wood becomes food for termites, wood-boring beetles, and a host of decomposers. By breaking down dead material, these plants and animals play an essential role in the recycling of nutrients and minerals back to the soil, where they can nourish a whole new generation of growth.

Several species of shade-tolerant trees persist in the moist, wooded areas beneath the evergreen canopy, including Giant Chinquapin, Canyon Live Oak, Pacific Dogwood, California Bay, and Madrone, whose red skin has the look and feel of smooth adobe walls. Huckleberry, a member of the heath family, is also present and is a common understory companion to the redwoods on the preserve. The leafy patches provide ideal habitat for the Dusky-footed Wood Rat, also known as the packrat. It builds hogans within the thickets and feeds on the edible berries, as do birds, Gray Fox, Striped and Spotted skunks, and Deer Mice, so named for their oversized ears. Predators, such as the Northern Goshawk and Spotted Owl, rely on the small creatures for food.

The forest is punctuated by clearings that resulted from some form of disturbance, either natural or manmade. The Kato Indians systematically burned limited areas of the preserve to encourage growth of the grasses and shrubs that provided them with nuts, berries, and seeds; these clearings attracted deer as well. In small areas, white settlers removed redwoods for lumber. Opening up the forest canopy allowed such sun-loving shrubs as Whitethorn and California Coffeeberry to become established. Soil conditions, light availability, and moisture have also affected the vegetation mix at the preserve. Growing conditions are more restrictive on dry, exposed sites.

An amazing contrast cloaks the opposite sides of many ridges. The preserve's annual rainfall, at 130 inches, is identical to such wet spots as Singapore and Guatemala City. The moist Douglas-fir forest thrives on the shady, north-facing slopes, but chaparral, a community of leathery-leaved shrubs (more at home in a 15-inch-per-year rainfall), covers the hot, south-facing ridges. Because almost all of the annual precipitation falls in winter, the sunny ridges dry out thoroughly during the annual summer drought and foster the blanket of chaparral.

In the large meadows that dot the preserve comes the sound of rasping, snapping cicadas. California Poppy, Common Yarrow, lupine, Woodland Star, and Blue Dicks bloom in fields of Wild Oat-grass and Wild Rye Grass. From thickets of flowering California Lilac waft smells reminiscent of a grandmother's bottle of favorite perfume.

The vegetation mix changes dramatically along the banks of the Eel River and its feeder streams. White Alder, Oregon Ash, Western Yew, Elk's Clover, and a variety of ferns contribute to a lush streamside plant community. A large and varied population of animals also depends on the year-round water. Among the riparian dwellers are the Pacific Giant Salamander, Mink, Raccoon, and Fisher.

The River Otter is also found at streamside. This sleek-bodied, furry animal is well adapted to the aquatic habitat. The river supplies it with crayfish, garter snakes, frogs, and fish for food; the forest offers hollow logs for denning. River Otters are a hoot to watch. They love to frolic in the river, sliding down its smooth, steep banks, swimming gracefully in the clear water, and chasing each other across the rocks.

The preserve is home to a large number of birds. During the spring migration, you might spot one of North America's most tropically colored birds, the Lazuli Bunting. Ravens and Turkey Vultures ride the updrafts over the meadows, while Black Phoebes build mud-and-straw

Northern California Coast Range Preserve ▶

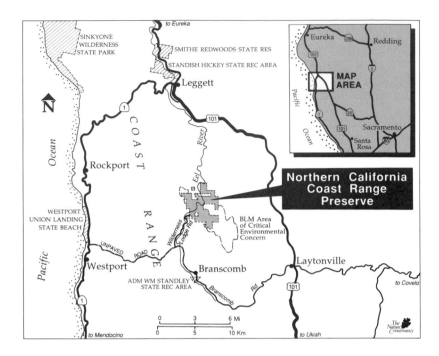

nests in the rafters of the abandoned homesteads below. In the forest, Black-headed Grosbeaks call, along with Solitary Vireos, Chestnut-backed Chickadees, Orange-crowned Warblers, and Wilson's Warblers, to name just a few.

One preserve resident, the feral pig, has become a destructive force. The pigs are the legacy of the early settlers. Around the turn of the century they either escaped from captivity or were allowed to roam free. They quickly reverted to a wild condition. The amazingly adaptable animals eat almost anything in sight. Using their snouts and tusks as plows, they root through the fragile soils in the meadows in search of bulbs, mushrooms, small rodents, insects, reptiles, and amphibians. After the pigs finish feeding, the ground looks as if it's been rototilled. The stripped soil is quickly colonized by such introduced weeds as Turkey Mullein, Red Brome, and Soft Chess that inhibit the growth of native grasses and herbs.

Other large mammals on the preserve include the Gray Fox, Black-tailed Mule Deer, Coyote, Mountain Lion, and Badger. Black Bears are also present. While you're hiking, look for their claw marks in the bark of Madrone trees. The deep scratches signal whose territory is whose, and remind us that the old-growth forest truly does belong to wildlife.

Northern California Coast Range Checklist

INFORMATION

For information, call (707) 984-6653, or write to The North Coast Range Preserve, 42101 Wilderness Lodge Road, Branscomb, CA 95417.

SIZE

7,520 acres

SEASONAL HIGHLIGHTS

Year-round wildlife sightings; spring and fall bird migration; and spring wildflowers.

WEATHER

Annual rainfall averages 130 inches; cool and foggy mornings fall through spring.

ON-SITE FACILITIES

Information kiosk, hiking trails, and picnic tables. Overnight camping available for pre-arranged research and educational groups only.

NEAREST OFF-SITE FACILITIES

19.9 miles away via two-lane road to Laytonville

EQUIPMENT

good walking shoes
rain jacket
binoculars
food and water

TIME REQUIRED

Full day

DIRECTIONS

The preserve is located in Mendocino County, 150 miles north of San Francisco via Highway 101. From Laytonville, turn west on the Branscomb Road and drive to Branscomb — 13.9 miles. Three miles past Branscomb turn north on Wilderness Lodge Road and go another three miles. The preserve headquarters is at the end of the road.

Northern Spotted Owl

Strix occidentalis caurina

DISTINCTIVE WHITE spots on a background of dark brown feathers give the Spotted Owl its name. The 20-inch-long bird sports foot-long wings and a round face with no ear tufts. Its dark brown eyes are piercing. Its high-pitched hooting sounds like a small dog barking.

There are three subspecies of Spotted Owl. The Northern is restricted to the forests from Marin County north to British Columbia. The California is found primarily in the Sierra Nevada and the Coast Range from Monterey to San Diego. The Mexican occurs from southern Utah to central Mexico.

These owls are hard to find; little is known about their demography. Adults seem to be long-lived, whereas juvenile survival appears extremely low. A study recently conducted in the North Coast area, for instance, revealed that eight out of ten fledglings died their first year.

The species is thought to be monogamous and to mate for life. Like most owls, Spotteds don't build nests, but use naturally occurring sites. Favorite locations are the broken crowns of trees or the cavities of rotted trunks. Old-growth forests (composed of trees from seedlings to two hundred years or older) offer more nesting opportunities. The resulting snags and downed woody debris also provide cover and habitat for Flying Squirrels and Dusky-footed Wood Rats, the owl's major prey.

This dependence on old-growth forest has made the Spotted Owl extremely vulnerable and, consequently, extremely imperiled. The bird's habitat is shrinking at an alarming rate. Fewer than five million acres remain of the original fifteen million acres of old-growth forest in California, Oregon, and Washington. Even that is disappearing fast. Approximately 50,000 acres of timber are being harvested every year.

Experts say the loss of habitat has led to a drastic decline in population. No more than 4,000 to 6,000 Northern Spotted Owls are es-

Northern Spotted Owl

Keith Hansen 1987

timated to survive. To compare current densities with historic ones is difficult, but the California Department of Fish and Game figures that of the state's estimated 2,100 historical Spotted Owl territories, only 1,317 are left. And recently, pairs have been seen in only forty-seven percent of the known habitat sites.

As the owl's habitat becomes fragmented, additional stress is placed on the species' genetic pool. What's more, clear-cut forests are an open invitation to the Spotted Owl's primary predator, the Great Horned Owl. Barred Owls, a competitor, are also finding their way into the deep forest, a domain once reserved for this rare and unusual bird.

FOUR

Vina Plains

Vernal Splendor

IN THE heat of August, Vina Plains looks scorched and parched. The sparse brown covering of dried grass appears to hold little promise. But what a change come spring. The rains of autumn and winter release a sea of green blades splashed with showy masses of wildflowers. Layers of white, yellow, and blue surround vernal pools like bathtub rings. And for a few fleeting weeks, Vina explodes in a burst of new life.

Located thirteen miles north of Chico, Vina Plains Preserve is a rarity in the Great Central Valley. The land has never been plowed. It is one of those few patches of virgin grassland that still exist in California—only one percent of the state's historic total survives. Though cattle eventually replaced the Tule Elk and Pronghorn that once roamed the area, Vina remains relatively untrampled.

As a result, the preserve supports a floristic assemblage that has been extirpated in most other parts of the state. No fewer than 280 species of plants grow here, offering excellent examples of adaptation to the Mediterranean climate, and five of these plants are considered rare: Fremont's Calycadenia, Hoover Spurge, Greene's Orcuttia, Hairy Orcuttia, and Slender Orcuttia. The two distinct plant communities—Northern Basalt Vernal Pool and Cismontane Light Soil Flower Field—have been given the highest protection priority ranking by the California Natural Diversity Data Base.

Vina Plains owes its distinctive flora to a rich geological past. The impervious, rocky hardpan was formed by volcanic mudflows in the foothills a million or more years ago. Later—about 100,000 years ago—weathering weakened the cementlike fanglomerate and converted the rock back to sand, gravel, and eventually clay. Then, 80,000 to 90,000

Vina Plains Preserve ▶

years later, sand and silt, carried either by wind during the glacial period or by flooding from the Sacramento River system, were deposited in the area of the preserve. Strong winds and dry climate worked in concert to remove the upper deposit of soil and to scour vernal pools into the weakened fanglomerate.

The underlying impermeable layer of clay allows vernal pools to fill with rainwater in winter, and the only way this water escapes is through evaporation. For plant life at the pools, this means being drowned for part of the year and baking for the rest. Some native plants have adapted to these special conditions. Following summer aestivation, the annual plants germinate and perennials sprout, blooming in concentric rings of color when the ponds dry.

Three types of rare orcutt grass are among the many plants that rely on this unique habitat. Each has adapted to withstand the wildly fluctuating conditions—drought in summer, flood in winter. Hairy Orcuttia, for instance, secretes a sticky, aromatic substance that, apparently, helps it survive during dry times and protects it against herbivory.

Many of the vernal pool plants have been severely restricted in range from loss of habitat. Greene's Orcuttia, which once grew in eight California counties, is found today in only three. Hoover Spurge, another unusual inhabitant of large, clay-lined vernal pools, is known from Tehama to Tulare County, but is protected only on the Vina Plains Preserve.

Vernal pools also support a distinctive assemblage of invertebrates. One species of snail burrows into the pond sediments when the waters begin to recede and spends summer beneath the soil surface. Numerous crustaceans live in the shallow waters. Larger ones include fairy shrimp, tadpole shrimp, and clam shrimp, all having numerous leaflike legs. Fairy shrimp are light-colored filter feeders, often observed swimming gracefully near the surface when the pools are cold. Tadpole shrimp are bottom-dwellers that generally feed on any dead material they encounter. Mature clam shrimp stay near the bottom where they filter-feed on organic particles and tiny organisms. Each type hatches from eggs that must first survive the summer drought before being stimulated by cold rainwater flooding into the vernal pool depressions. They quickly grow to maturity and deposit their own eggs, which settle on the pond sediments to remain throughout the summer.

Migratory waterfowl and shorebirds flock to the pools to feed on these tiny invertebrates. Ringing the shoreline are Great Egret, Great Blue Heron, Greater Yellowlegs, Black-necked Stilt, and Killdeer. Tundra Swan, Snow and Canada geese, American Wigeon, Mallard, and Pintail paddle around on the surface.

The second plant community, Cismontane Light Soil Flower Field, is characterized by thin soils that support perennial herbs, annual forbs,

Purple Needlegrass

and native and introduced grasses. Because the soils generally produce only a thin cover of grass, the spring display of wildflowers is consistently more showy here than in other parts of the state.

From February to May, Vina Plains is brilliant with alternating waves of blooms. Among the more colorful flowering plants are White-flowered Navarretia, Adobe Lily, Ithuriel's Spear, and Meadowfoam. A large variety of families is represented: Crowfoot, Mallow, Geranium, Violet, Poppy, Mustard, Primrose, Pea, and Snapdragon are only a few.

Providing a verdant backdrop to the dollops of color are numerous grass species, including such natives as Purple Needlegrass, Western Witchgrass, and Pacific Bluegrass. But like all California grassland areas, Vina Plains is not free of alien invaders. The ubiquitous Soft Chess and Red Brome are firmly established.

However, the cover of grass is sparse, offering little protection for mammals. Consequently, population and diversity are low. The most populous animal is the Deer Mouse, followed by Botta Pocket Gopher, and Black-tailed Hare.

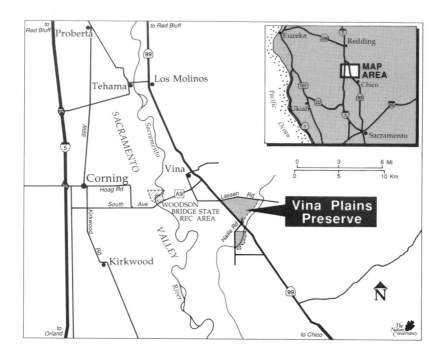

Not surprisingly, the rodents attract a fair share of predators, including Northern Harriers and Red-tailed Hawks. Prairie Falcons have been sighted here; so have Bald Eagles, which use Vina as a wintering area.

But generally speaking, Vina is not attractive to many perching birds. The flat, treeless topography holds little interest for arboreal species. Mostly what you'll find are field feeders, such as Horned Lark, Western Meadowlark, Savannah Sparrow, and Brewer's Blackbird.

This openness gives Vina Plains its special beauty. The low relief, absence of roads and utility corridors, and sparse herbaceous growth all contribute to a sense of wide-open naturalness. In this day and age, that is a rare commodity in itself.

Vina Plains Checklist

INFORMATION

Docent-guided tours are conducted each Saturday and Sunday morning from the first of March to the middle of May or until the ponds have dried. Group tours may be arranged for other times. For more information, contact the Management Docent Chair/Tour Coordinator at (916) 891-8462.

SIZE

1,950 acres

SEASONAL HIGHLIGHTS

Wildflower display from March through May; vernal pools and migrating waterfowl, December through April.

WEATHER

Mediterranean climate with dry summers. Rain, accompanied by strong south winds, in late fall and winter. Winds are from the west or northwest.

ON-SITE FACILITIES

None

NEAREST OFF-SITE FACILITIES

13 miles south in Chico

EQUIPMENT

good walking shoes
binoculars
food and water
magnifying glass

TIME REQUIRED

3 hours

DIRECTIONS

The preserve is located at the southern edge of Tehama County bordering Highway 99, 13 miles north of Chico. The entry gate is on the east side of the highway, approximately one-third mile north of Singer Creek and opposite Haille Road.

Boggs Lake

Poolside Beauty

MOST PEOPLE think of North Carolina swamps as habitat for carnivorous plants, but California has its own versions. Boggs Lake, a pocket-size preserve a hundred miles north of San Francisco, is home to Bladderwort, a yellow snapdragon-like flower with feathery leaves that's as voracious as any Venus's Flytrap. In spring, golden sheets of Bladderwort cover lake waters, imprisoning aquatic creatures in tiny, bladderlike traps that provide this carnivore with added nourishment.

Bladderwort is only one of the unusual plants that keeps this 141-acre woodland oasis imbued with blooms through summer. Several species grow here and in only a few other places in the world; a couple are considered rare and endangered.

Boggs Lake lies eight miles south of Clear Lake in a million-year-old lava flow near the base of Mount Hannah on the eastern flank of the Mayacamas Mountains. Pomo and Yuki Indians used it as a hunting ground and source of water prior to the arrival of white settlers in gold rush days.

The lake is named after Henry Carrol Boggs, an early pioneer who established a lumber mill beside the lake in 1868. At one time, Boggs decided to deepen the lake by setting off a blast in the middle. The explosion created a hole that acted like a drain in a bathtub. All the water immediately poured out, leaving the lakebed dry.

The disappearance of the water attests to the lake's volcanic origin. It is underlain by underground caverns left by lava flows. The loss of water forced Boggs to close the mill for two years until he could plug the hole and let the basin fill with water again.

In truth, Boggs Lake isn't a lake but a vernal pool, a shallow depression in an impervious layer of clay left unfilled by lava flow. The pool

Boggs Lake Preserve

is not fed by springs or streams, but acts as a catch basin for rainfall and runoff from the surrounding watershed. The water evaporates in summer.

Thousands of tiny, jewel-like vernal pools once dotted California, predominantly in the Great Central Valley, but agriculture and development have left only a few. Boggs Lake differs from others that remain in the valley — it is not set in grassland, but rather in a forest of Douglas-fir, Ponderosa Pine, California Black Oak, and Madrone.

The lake's peculiar geological and hydrogeological conditions give rise to a unique botanical life. A distinctive and highly localized plant community has evolved to survive the pool's extreme seasonal variation in moisture, a water level that can fluctuate as many as twelve feet within a few seasons.

When the lake water starts to recede, wildflowers bloom in concentric rings around the shrinking pool, creating a kaleidoscope of color. Two species are listed as endangered: the hard-to-find Hedge Hyssop and the Many-flowered Navarretia. Hedge Hyssop is neither a hedge, nor does it have any known medicinal purpose like the hyssop mentioned frequently in the Bible. It stands about six inches high and sports a peculiar-looking flower that has a yellow tube and white petals. Only a few of these plants are found each year. The Many-flowered Navarretia grows in little mounds an inch high and three to four inches across. In

Downningia bicornuta

spring, its sky-blue blossoms become so dense they make lakeshore resemble lake. Other Navarretias, as yet unidentified, also grow on the lakebed.

Two kinds of bright blue Downingia cover the lakebed while waves of Slender Orcutt Grass display purple seedheads. Indian Lovevine blooms in a tangle of orange, silklike threads and orange blossoms. This parasite grows on other plants and winds itself around them. As soon as the lovevine finds it can get away with living off another, it discards its own roots and lower parts and takes all nourishment from the host.

In the open water you'll find Watershield, a secretive plant that opens its reddish-purple flowers only on two successive days of the year. The Watershield pushes its flowers above the water to receive pollen, closes the blooms, and pulls them back under the surface. The next day, the flowers are pushed up again and opened to dispel their own pollen before being closed and resubmerged. Under water, the plant goes to work forming seeds. The Watershield's leaves are covered with a gelatinous layer so unusual in composition that specimens have been sent off to a botanist in Czechoslovakia for study.

Boggs Lake's unique plant community has established the site as a significant botanical locality. Spurred by reports of a proposed development at the site, the California Native Plant Society urged The Nature

Conservancy to acquire the lake and its immediate surroundings. In 1972, the Conservancy persuaded the property's owner, The Fibreboard Corporation, a forest products firm, to donate 101 acres. In 1986 an additional 40 acres were acquired.

The latest acquisition comprises a meadow and oak and pine woodlands. It supports a variety of wildlife, including such mammals as Bobcat, Black-tailed Mule Deer, Mountain Lion, Raccoon, Striped Skunk, and squirrels. A number of migrant songbirds rely on it as do many different resident species. All told, 142 species of birds have been identified. Western Bluebird hovers over the open meadow; Pileated, Downy, and Hairy woodpeckers tap the trees for insects. Brown Creeper, Violet-green Swallow, and Purple Martin nest in the mixed forest. Poorwill occasionally nest in the dry, rocky edges of the meadow. Several species of migrant warblers forage in the area.

The open water of the preserve attracts plenty of waterfowl in winter. Coot and Red-winged Blackbird frequent the tules while Mallard, Wood Duck, and Hooded Merganser paddle on the ponds. Osprey and Bald Eagle arrive in winter to feed on fish.

Carp and catfish are present when the lake is deep enough to support fish. They were introduced into the lake earlier in the century. Though the lake nearly dries up in summer, a couple of shallow pools usually survive each year. The dead carcasses of carp are food for the Raven and Turkey Vulture. Great Blue Heron spear frogs and other amphibians along the shore, while Green-backed Heron and Wilson's Phalarope migrate through. In the manzanita growing along the banks, you can spot the Willow Flycatcher darting for meals. Listen for the Olive-sided Flycatcher higher in the trees.

Late spring and early summer offer the best views of the sequence of flowering that ensues as the lake dries. These seasons also bring the peak of bird activity. Both flora and fauna are strongly affected by the water level in the lake. Substantial fluctuations in lake level make each year different in terms of what you'll see.

The preserve has no facilities. Access is gained through tours scheduled from April to June. From the entrance, walk clockwise following the shore—that way you won't miss the best parts of this surprisingly complex ecosystem. Don't let the preserve's size deter you. Compared to others, it appears quite small, and for that matter, so do its unusual resident plants.   But in the world of botany, Boggs Lake is a giant.

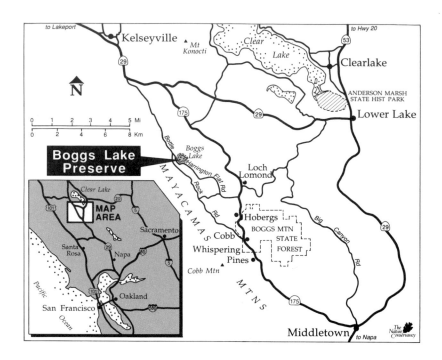

Boggs Lake Checklist

INFORMATION

For information, contact The Nature Conservancy, 785 Market St., 3rd Floor, San Francisco, CA 94103; (415) 777-0487.

SIZE

141 acres

SEASONAL HIGHLIGHTS

Wildflower display from early May to mid-June.

WEATHER

Mediterranean, with hot summers and moderate winters. Annual rainfall is 64 inches with occasional snow.

ON-SITE FACILITIES

None

NEAREST OFF-SITE FACILITIES

6.5 miles in small mountain community of Cobb

EQUIPMENT

comfortable walking shoes
binoculars
water
magnifying glass

TIME REQUIRED

3 hours

DIRECTIONS

From San Francisco Bay Area, take Interstate 80 to Vallejo and head north on Highway 29 for 58 miles to Highway 175 in Middleton. Take 175 northeast 10 miles to Cobb. Turn left at Bottle Rock Road and go northeast for 6.5 miles. Watch carefully on right for Harrington Flat Road. Turn right and go one mile. Lake is on the left. Park on left shoulder at preserve entrance.

Fairfield Osborn

Chaotic Waters

GUESS AGAIN if you think Mount Lassen is the closest volcanic mountain to San Francisco. Just sixty miles north lies Sonoma Mountain, a volcanic ridge formed less than seven million years ago. At one time enormous fissures vented huge quantities of molten lava, while spectacular eruptions scattered ash and debris for miles. The mountain later uplifted into place. Though it is quiet today, rocks are still warm only a few hundred feet below the surface.

Sonoma Mountain's geological heritage makes for some unusual inhabitants. The chance deposits of ash and flow lava have cooked up a veritable slumgullion stew of biological communities. You can get a taste of this diversity by visiting the 210-acre preserve located on the western slope. Covered with oaks and evergreens and patches of chaparral and grassland, the preserve is sliced by a perennial stream and its four tributaries. Riparian communities thrive wherever the waters flow. Nearly three hundred vascular plant species grow here, presenting a nonstop show of color. Some of these plants are rare.

Flora isn't the only rarity found at the preserve. The main waterway, Copeland Creek, is unlike any other perennial deciduous stream that occurs below snow level in California. Huge boulders, crashing like distant thunderclaps, roll downstream in its unstable bed during winter storms. Anything in the way of these rolling stones is crushed. As a result, no fish swim in its waters, and their predatory absence has allowed an incredible diversity of invertebrate life to thrive. More than 150 insect species inhabit the stream system, including a rare aquatic sowbug, the California Eyed Asellid, which exists here and at only three other sites in the world.

Amphibians and reptiles are also present in large numbers — the

Fairfield Osborn Preserve ▶

TRAIL
GUIDES

thirty-one different species include the voracious Pacific Giant Salamander, Western Pond Turtle, Red-legged Frog, and several types of snakes, including Western Rattlesnake. Over eighty Western Pond Turtles have been counted sunning themselves all at once at Cattail Pond.

A steady succession of flora blooms in the varied habitats that cover the slopes. During winter, delicate Veined White Butterflies sip nectar from the early blooming California Milkmaid. The Lobb's Buttercup — a species considered rare — appears in the vernal pool in spring and gives off a vanilla-like aroma. Giant Trillium, Miniature Lupine, and Shooting Star go wild. In June the native California grasses turn brown, though Gold Nuggets and tarweed provide a summery splash of yellow. By evening the night-opening Soap Plant unfurls. Pollinating hummingbirds attend crimson-petaled California Fuchsia, which burst into autumn displays in the mountainside chaparral.

Miwok Indians lived here for thousands of years. Shell middens and arrowhead chippings of obsidian can still be seen. The Europeans who later came to work the land left behind graceful stone walls. In 1972, the site was donated to the Nature Conservancy by its owners, William and Joan Roth, and is named after Joan's father, Fairfield Osborn, former president of the New York Zoological Society and author of such seminal works on ecology as *Our Plundered Planet* and *Limits of the Earth*.

The preserve is a fitting memorial to the late conservationist who dedicated his life to educating others about the importance of protecting the environment. It serves as an outdoor classroom and field laboratory for biology students from nearby Sonoma State University and for the 1,500 fifth-grade students who participate each year in the preserve's environmental education program.

A small interpretive center located near the preserve's entrance is open most weekends and is the logical place to begin a tour. You'll find descriptive displays with color photographs, taxidermy mounts, vertebrate charts, live animals, an herbarium, and an extensive insect collection. From here you can follow the well-marked, self-guided nature trail.

The trail begins by crossing Courtship Creek, a splendid spot to pause and investigate an aquatic ecosystem up close. At the bottom of the stream, immature mayflies, stoneflies, and caddisflies scrape algae off the rocks and feed on creatures smaller than themselves. These aquatic bugs eventually metamorphose into short-lived, winged adults that mate along the stream or in swarms above the creekbed.

The trail parallels the creek as it cuts through the rich volcanic soil. To the right is a patch of rolling grassland aptly named Butterfly Meadow. Chocolate-brown Mourning Cloak butterflies frequent the meadow in spring, while later in the season Buckeye and California Sister butterflies arrive. In late summer and fall, blooming flowers attract nectar-seeking Monarchs and Tiger Swallowtails.

At Fairfield Osborn, half of the more than forty varieties of grass are native. An intricate web of wildlife depends on the grassy habitat for survival. Grasshoppers feed on the blades. In turn, they become an important food source for Western Fence Lizard, Alligator Lizard, Western Racer, and other reptiles. Bluebirds swoop off fencepost perches to snap up hungry 'hoppers; so do sharp-eyed Kestrels, which dive from the sky. Two birds that nest in the grassland are the Mourning Dove and California Quail. Their eggs are prized by a number of stealthy carnivores, including Raccoon, Long-tailed Weasel, and Striped Skunk.

On the left side of Courtship Creek lies an expanse of marshland larger than a football field. The tangle of nettle, sedge, and rush provides a home for the secretive Sora and Virginia Rail. Walk to the edge of the marsh and clap your hands. Sometimes the rails will answer with a call that sounds like a cross between a laugh and the noise pigs make slurping slop.

At the eastern tip of the marsh is a crescent-shaped pond filled with tules and shaded by a stately Weeping Willow, an eastern species planted by early homesteaders. Tiny Duckweed covers the water. The willow's trunks have been punctured by Red-breasted Sapsuckers, which feed on the exuding sap and the insects it attracts.

Farther along the trail you'll reach Cattail Pond. Flocks of Red-winged Blackbirds roost in the cattails along with insect-grabbing Black Phoebes. The pond was made to serve as a reservoir, but it encourages plenty of native wildlife. Besides the large contingency of Western Pond Turtles, there are Red-legged Frogs and Rough-skinned Newts. Wood Ducks and Mallards feed on plants and mosquito larvae. Damselflies and dragonflies patrol overhead in search of insect prey.

From here, the trail loops back along Trillium Creek to its confluence with the main channel of Copeland Creek. It passes through the preserve's largest plant community, Oak Woodland. The acorns from Coast Live Oak, Black Oak, and Oregon Oak are a dietary staple of Black-tailed Mule Deer and such rodents as Western Gray Squirrel and Deer Mouse. Other trees growing in the woodland are California Bay, whose aromatic leaves release a pungent fragrance when crushed, and Buckeye, whose white flowers suggest candelabras at a formal wedding.

An interesting feature of the oak trees are oak galls, bizarre structures that grow directly out of the leaves and twigs. From minute to almost baseball-sized, galls are produced by the tree in response to chemicals injected by small insects—the Gall Wasp and Gall Fly—when they lay their eggs. The larvae live inside the gall, feeding on the plant tissues rich in proteins and carbohydrates. Some birds have learned how to break the galls apart to get at the soft-bodied, immature insects inside.

Fairfield Osborn's oak woodlands are filled with birds. Brown Creepers walk up trunks and pry for food under the bark with their slender, down-curved bills. Flocks of Plain Titmouse, Chestnut-backed Chickadee, and Common Bushtit flit through the forest, combing the foliage for bugs. Steller's Jays and Scrub Jays scold noisily from branches, while various species of flycatcher dart out from the edges of the forest in pursuit of fleeing insects. At night, Screech Owls and Great Horned Owls take to the air.

The preserve's Riparian Forest community flourishes in a narrow band on the banks of Copeland Creek and its tributaries. White Alder is the dominant tree species. Flocks of Pine Siskin pass through the region in late spring and pry seeds from the tree's conelike fruits. Look straight up and you can see them hanging upside down in the alder canopy. Beneath the alders and Big-leaf Maples grows a tropical-looking understory of Wood, Shield, and Sword ferns. Polypody Ferns sprout from the hulks of old logs and moss-covered rocks.

The forest floor here is littered with leaves, limbs, and logs. Underneath them is a squirming, crawling community of centipedes, millipedes, and termites. Fungus clings to the rotting wood. Slime mold, resembling human hair or wisps of colored cotton, occurs sporadically on the tops of fallen logs.

The trail eventually emerges from the riparian forest and skirts between a patch of grassland and oak woodland. This ecotone—a place where two plant communities overlap—is a good place to look for owls and hawks. Cooper's, Red-tailed, and Sharp-shinned hawks, Golden Eagle, and Turkey Vulture soar through the skies.

Off in the distance, a stand of 150-foot-high Douglas-firs towers over the oak woodland. This is a front line for one of nature's battlegrounds. The firs are fighting to become the dominant biotic community on the preserve at the expense of the oaks.

Each adult Douglas-fir sends out thousands of tiny seeds. Spread by breezes, they take root in the oak woodland where they wait for a break in the canopy. Once they get the chance, these fast-growing firs shoot skyward, blocking sunlight from the shorter oaks. A large deer population also helps the firs: Deer eat acorns and almost all of the oak saplings, but they only feed on the newest green foliage of the conifers, leaving the bulk of saplings to survive. The recent lack of fire favors the firs as well.

But don't count the oaks out yet. Because beetle damage is claiming some of the oldest firs, the oak trees are able to withstand the invasion. Only time will tell which tree will win the battle. The preserve, in the meantime, guarantees a place for the struggle to continue.

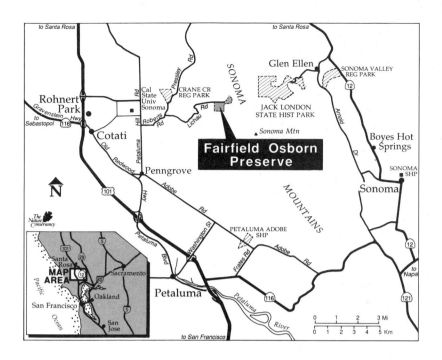

Fairfield Osborn Checklist

INFORMATION

Fairfield Osborn is open during daylight hours on weekends only. For more information, including maps and brochures on request, and to make advance arrangements, contact the preserve's office at 6543 Lichau Rd., Penngrove, CA 94951; (707) 795-5069.

SIZE

210 acres

SEASONAL HIGHLIGHTS

Year-round wildflower display; spring and fall bird migration.

WEATHER

Mediterranean, with hot and dry summers; mild, damp winters. Average annual rainfall is 30 inches.

ON-SITE FACILITIES

Interpretive center and self-guided nature trail.

NEAREST OFF-SITE FACILITIES

6 miles away in Cotati

EQUIPMENT

good walking shoes
binoculars
food and water
sun protection

TIME REQUIRED

3 to 4 hours

DIRECTIONS

From San Francisco, take Highway 101 north through Petaluma to the Cotati exit (Sonoma State exit). Follow East Cotati Road to Petaluma Hill Road. Turn right and go about one-half mile to Roberts Road. Left on Roberts, then right on Lichau Road. When almost to the end of Lichau Road, stop at parking area by mailbox 6543.

SEVEN

Ring Mountain
Room with a View

FROM EMERALD to aquamarine, and every shade in between, Ring Mountain glows green in spring. A thick weave of verdant native bunchgrass cloaks the mountainsides. Boulders are splashed with lichen the color of lime. Even the bare dirt on the mountain exposed by hiking trails is green—a powdery till ground fine by boot and hoof.

Located in Marin County on the northern end of the Tiburon Peninsula and just fifteen miles north of downtown San Francisco, Ring Mountain is that rarest of things: open space abounding with wildlife close to the urban core.

Also unusual are seven species of plants classified by the California Native Plant Society as rare or endangered. These plants, found on the mountain's flanks, are botanical endemics restricted to serpentine soil, and they blossom in succession from early spring through midsummer. The most famous is the Tiburon Mariposa Lily, showing a spectacular flower with tan, cinnamon, and yellow bowl-shaped petals, that blooms here and nowhere else on earth.

In addition to plants, Ring Mountain claims two other rarities: lawsonite, a mineral discovered on the mountain in 1895 by famed University of California geologist Andrew Lawson, and a tiny species of Blind Harvestman spider, or daddy-longlegs, *Sitalcina tiburona*. The spider lives under the mountain's serpentine rocks and is not known to exist anywhere else.

Ring Mountain is a favorite among wildflower fanciers, hikers, geologists, and historians, but clearly it has been luring people up its slopes for millennia. Circular petroglyphs chipped in the face of an outcropping of rocks near the peak were inscribed by an Indian culture as long ago as 2,000 years. Though no one knows for sure what significance these curious carvings had, archaeologists conjecture that the site may

have been used as a sort of Stonehenge, a sacred place where coastal Indians performed rituals to ensure the productivity of the fertile baylands below, the source of so much of their food. Other evidence shows pre-Hispanic human activity on the mountain, including a bedrock mortar used for grinding acorns gathered from nearby oaks and a smattering of long-abandoned campsites.

The site is part of the first Spanish land grant made north of the Golden Gate. Rancho Corte de Madera del Presidio, which also included parts of what are present-day Mill Valley, Corte Madera, and Larkspur, was given by Governor Jose Figueroa of Alta California in 1834 to John Thomas Reed, a colorful Dubliner who had judiciously married Hilaria Sanchez, daughter of the Commandante of the Presidio.

Their rancho became a major source of beef for the growing Bay Area. It also served as the rail corridor for a freight line linking San Francisco and Humboldt Bay. Hardly a trace remains, however, of the late, great Northwestern Pacific Railroad.

At the turn of the century, the mountain acquired its name from George E. Ring, a county supervisor who lived nearby. Later, the U.S. Army commandeered the peak and installed an antiaircraft installation on its easterly knoll. When intercontinental ballistics made the 90 mm antiaircraft cannons obsolete, the army abandoned the site.

Suburbanization started creeping up the mountain's sides after World War II. A neighborhood group intent on protecting the area brought the rare local species to public attention. The Nature Conservancy acquired title to 117 acres and expanded the preserve to 377 acres by 1985. A comprehensive, integrated management program followed, which addresses the need for protection, restoration, research, education, and public use.

The area has a long history of educational use by elementary and high schools and colleges of the Bay Area; it gets frequent use by environmental classes and field researchers. And the mountain's rare flora receive the keen attention of visiting botanists.

These plants, called "serpentine endemics," are the product of decaying serpentine, an unusual mineral that has weathered to produce a thin, gravelly soil peppered with rocks and small boulders. Serpentine is low in essential nutrients, but high in magnesium and heavy metals. This combination makes life very difficult for most plant species. The plants that have adapted to survive in this environment have become so specialized they can no longer compete in other habitats, but flourish in serpentine soil.

Tiburon Paintbrush, for one, grows only on serpentine. Like other paintbrushes, the petals of this species are hidden within the showy bracts and lemon-yellow-tipped calyces. A shrubby perennial that

◄ *Ring Mountain Preserve*

grows one to two feet tall, it has compact flower spikes that bloom from March to May in just a few places on the ridges.

Other unusual serpentine plants include Marin Dwarf Flax. This delicately branched annual blends easily into the drying grasses of late spring. Its small, pale rose-to-white petals don't last long. Tiburon Tarweed is a glandular, aromatic annual with silver-gray, grasslike leaves and clear-yellow flowers that are arranged in small, tight heads typical of the Sunflower family. The inconspicuous flowers of the Tiburon Buckwheat are borne on bare stems. Bright rose-red and tiny, they grow in clumps of small balls. Serpentine Reedgrass, a perennial, grows among the scattered rocks. Its long, narrow leaves gracefully arch to form robust mounds.

Geologists also flock to Ring Mountain to see some of the most unusual rock types in the Bay Area. The mountain is capped by serpentine in broad, sheetlike masses ten to fifty feet thick. Underlying the serpentine is a chaotic mixture of various types of rock known collectively as Franciscan melange. The mountain's base is a zone of weak, intensely sheared rock called melange matrix. Included are blocks of serpentine, greenstone, sandstone, and chert, as well as bodies of rare and exotic metamorphic rock, including ecologites, amphibolites, and coarse-grained schists. Some of the rocks in this zone are of such unusual mineral composition and massive texture that none of the standard rock names apply.

To appreciate firsthand Ring Mountain's special geology and the assemblage of unique flora it supports, take the main trail at the preserve's entrance on Paradise Drive. The trail is well marked and easily switches back three-quarters of a mile from bayside up the north face to a fire road and the mountain's 602-foot-high summit.

The hike takes you over sweetwater freshets that spring from the mountainside and through a sea of knee-high native grasses thriving on sandstone soil, including California Oat-grass, Purple Needlegrass, and others. Their spreading crowns and bunchlike growth patterns provide food and cover for many kinds of small mammals and ground-nesting birds.

From March to May, the slope is dotted with delicate blooms of Oakland Star Tulips, their white petals touched with a blush of pink like fine white zinfandel. The lower portion of each petal has a raised gland covered by a membrane with a fringed border. In the summer you'll see only their dry, nodding capsules. Fat bumblebees plunder constellations of tiny yellow star-shaped flowers on the slope, while American Robins chase over patches of golden California Poppies.

The trail parallels channels of an intermittent stream cut into the mountain. Filled with a dark green canopy of California Bay, Madrone, and Coast Live Oak trees, the swales are punctuated in spring with the long, white flower clusters of scattered Buckeye trees. Deer, Gray Fox,

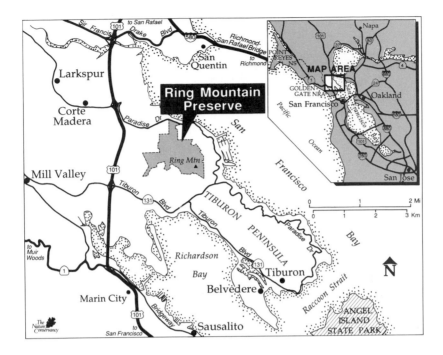

California Quail, and other fauna rely on the shady areas for cover. In the seeps and springs bloom Fontane Star Lily, delicate Hairgrass, and Seep-spring Monkeyflower.

Eventually the trail leads over the top of a stony ridge crowned by aptly named Turtle Rock and spotted by California Bay trees, whose contorted shapes are the result of persistent buffeting by coastal winds. The hiker's reward is a stunning view of the San Francisco Bay. Far below in Sausalito the masts of sailboats picketed in the harbor shimmer in the sun. Across the water the jagged skyline of San Francisco gleams white. The towers of the Golden Gate Bridge peek over the top of the Marin Headlands to the south.

Revolve slowly clockwise at this vantage point and you can trace the horizon as it rises along the silhouette of Mount Tamalpais then dips down to the towns of Corte Madera and Larkspur, travels along the ocher walls of San Quentin, crosses the Richmond-San Rafael Bridge, turns along the Berkeley Hills and descends to downtown Oakland where it crosses the Bay Bridge and winds up back in San Francisco again. As spectacular as this view is, the real beauty of the preserve lies in the continuation of rare species, species able to flourish in the midst of such a huge urban area.

Ring Mountain Checklist

Ring Mountain is open year-round during daylight hours. No permission is required to visit. For more information, contact the preserve's office at 3152 Paradise Drive, #101, Tiburon, CA 94920; (415) 435-6465.

SIZE

377 acres

SEASONAL HIGHLIGHTS

March through June for wild-flowers; spectacular views yearlong.

WEATHER

Fog is common. Coastal winds from the southwest are frequent. Rainfall averages 28 inches. No shade.

ON-SITE FACILITIES

Hiking trails

NEAREST OFF-SITE FACILITIES

1¾ miles to Corte Madera

EQUIPMENT

good walking shoes
binoculars
food and water

TIME REQUIRED

3 hours

DIRECTIONS

Ring Mountain is close at hand to all parts of the Bay Area. From San Francisco, take Highway 101 north to the Paradise Drive exit in Corte Madera. (Do not go to the town of Tiburon.) Follow Paradise Drive east for 1¾ miles. Just after Westward Drive is a fire road with a gate and sign on the right. Park off the pavement on the shoulder and walk to the hiking trail.

Tiburon Mariposa Lily

Calochortus tiburonensis

*T*HE TIBURON Mariposa Lily is known to grow naturally in only one spot in the world: Ring Mountain. This rare plant grows only on the serpentine soils high above the towns of Marin County.

So rare is this plant, in fact, that it went unnoticed and uncollected until 1973. After being recognized as a new species of *Calochortus* by Dr. Robert West, it was first described by Albert J. Hill. Given the lily's proximity to the urban Bay Area, it was a most remarkable discovery.

On the exposed, rocky upper slopes of Ring Mountain, the lily flourishes in high densities among boulders and bedrock, possibly as a result of the water regime associated with bare rock, or because it is less vulnerable to grazing, or both. Though mature plants are easily recognizable, it takes a trained eye to pick out the juveniles, which are often a sizeable portion of the population.

The Tiburon Mariposa Lily is a bulbous perennial characterized by a single persistent basal leaf that can reach about two feet high at full maturity. The basal leaf emerges a month or two after the onset of the winter rains—usually about mid-December. Seeds also sprout at this time. The flowering stalk appears above ground as early as the end of March, but more commonly throughout the first two weeks of April. Though larger individuals may produce as many as eight flowers and small plants only one, the average is two or three per reproducing adult. The plants reach full bloom by the last week in May and remain camouflaged in the drying grasses toward the end of June. The flower sets seed in mid-June to late-July.

The pollinator of this species is presently unknown. (The lily is self-incompatible, meaning that an individual cannot fertilize itself. It must exchange pollen with another plant.) Sweat Bees are a likely suspect; they are known to pollinate other rare species of mariposa lilies in simi-

Tiburon Mariposa Lily

lar windy climates, with similar nectar rewards, and with similar flower colors and patterns. Another possible pollinator is a crepuscular insect, one that is active only at dawn and dusk.

The Tiburon Mariposa Lily, while unknown from any other location in the world, is abundant at Ring Mountain Preserve. Black-tailed Mule Deer, Brush Rabbit, Betta Pocket Gopher, Black-tailed Hare, and other mammals use it for food, sometimes grazing on flower parts, thus preventing reproduction of individual plants for that year. Studies have begun to assess the population dynamics of this spectacular yet cryptic plant.

CENTRAL

EIGHT

Cosumnes River

Bayou Country

FIVE HOURS after a tide first rushes into the Golden Gate, its push is felt a hundred miles upstream on the lower Cosumnes River. Nothing impedes the flow. For that matter, nothing blocks the entire length of the river. That makes the Cosumnes unique. It is the largest undammed river in the entire Central Valley.

During winter rains, the Cosumnes may freely overflow its banks, thus supplying a heavy load of rich silt filled with valuable nutrients to adjacent wetlands and grasslands. The floodwaters create seasonal freshwater marshes that attract huge flocks of migratory waterfowl. Hundreds of threatened Lesser and Greater Sandhill cranes alight in winter, after the arrival of thousands of geese and ducks in fall. White-fronted, Canada, Ross', and Snow geese, Mallard, Cinnamon and Green-winged teals, Canvasback, and Ring-necked Duck are just a few of the species that rely on the Cosumnes, its sloughs, channels, and marshes, for food and shelter.

An even more outstanding natural feature of the Cosumnes is its Valley Oak Riparian Forest, the largest and highest quality stand in the state. Streamside Valley Oak forest is among the rarest of habitats in California. Riparian forests once covered 800,000 acres of the Central Valley, and Valley Oaks were a significant part. Today, the figure is one-hundredth of that. According to the California Natural Diversity Data Base, the Cosumnes's stand of 700 acres is the best of the 28 known stands of Valley Oak forest that survive.

The Valley Oak is among the largest oaks found anywhere in the world. It grows rapidly and can reach up to 12 feet in diameter and 150 feet tall. It is long-lived as well. Many of the large trees on the Cosumnes were present when John Sutter first explored the area.

These trees began to disappear shortly after the gold rush. Settlers recognized that the oaks grew on the richest, best watered soils; conse-

quently, forests were converted into farms and orchards. Because it was a main source of wood in a land of few trees, Valley Oak was cut for fuel and fenceposts. Thousands of acres were cut, corded, and shipped to San Francisco, where, until this century, the wood was used to heat houses. Oak also fired the boilers of steamboats on the Sacramento River.

The Valley Oaks that remain on the Cosumnes were spared because of frequent flooding. The forest is often inundated by water—mud lines at seven feet above ground are visible on the tree trunks.

Mixed in with the oaks are Oregon Ash (some of the tallest and finest found in the Central Valley), Box Elder, Fremont Cottonwood, and at least six species of willow. The trees form a leafy canopy that shades a lush understory of Elderberry, Snowberry, Mugwort, California Blackberry, and Poison-oak. Lianas of Wild Grape festoon the towering hardwoods, giving the forest an appearance John Muir described as "tropical luxuriance."

Raccoon, Black-tailed Mule Deer, Mink, Ringtail, and Virginia Opossum are several of the many mammals that call the forest home. The Pacific Tree Frog is common. Over 201 species of birds have been sighted on and around the preserve, including at least three pairs of Swainson's Hawk, a species listed by the state as threatened.

The preserve encompasses many other vegetation types. They generally correlate with topographic position, which serves as an indicator of flood frequency and duration. Mixed Riparian Forest lines the larger channels and occurs in frequently flooded areas. Valley Oak Woodland typically occurs at slightly higher elevations. Button-willow–Willow Thicket is found in poorly drained areas throughout the forested areas and at the lower margin of the slough channels. Several patches of Sandbar Willow also occur within the forested area. Freshwater Marsh vegetation (Tule, Cattail, pondweed, rush) is restricted to flat and annually flooded areas, whereas Grassland grows in high areas that flood infrequently and drain rapidly.

The preserve also includes agricultural land. A portion of the site was cultivated prior to being acquired by The Nature Conservancy—the preserve opened officially on May 30, 1987. In historic times fields were cleared, leveled, and planted with corn, grapes, and beans.

Today, the Conservancy is trying to turn back the clock and has embarked on an ambitious plan to reforest at least 200 acres with native Valley Oak. The effort entails recontouring the fields with machinery and planting by hand no fewer than 5,000 acorns gathered from the preserve's resident trees. The plan is to return the site to the condition it was in when Cosumnes Indians used to roam the area, hunting, fishing for salmon and steelhead that swam up the river, and collecting acorns.

◀ *Cosumnes River Preserve*

The sight of still water beneath the overhanging forests conjures up images of bayou country in the South. Indeed, there are similarities. The river is muddy and dark. Catfish and bass swim underneath while Muskrats snake across the surface. Green-backed Herons perch on low-lying limbs, and Wood Ducks dodge agilely between the trees.

Birds fill the forest with sound. Black-headed Grosbeaks play their flutelike song while Northern Orioles nesting along the banks scold. Nuttall's Woodpeckers tap for insects on the trunks of trees, and Western Tanagers mimic American Robins. From around each bend comes the quack of ducks. Gadwall, Northern Shoveler, and American Wigeon all stop by.

The banks of the Cosumnes are somewhat forbidding. Tangles of California Blackberry and the pink-blossomed California Wild Rose growing over downed willows and cottonwoods make hiking difficult, but levees provide good access through the marshes to the riverbanks and sloughs. One of the most common shrubs you'll first encounter is Button-willow. In June and July, the thickets blaze with white flowers that have the fragrance of freshly cut carnations.

Hike along the edges of the marsh and you'll find acres upon acres of watery ground carpeted by yellow-flowering Marsh Primrose. Powder-blue dragonflies and damselflies tipped with aquamarine hover over patches of Swamp Timothy, Swamp Knotweed, and Wapatoo, or Tule Potato. The colors of the marsh remain vibrant from early spring through late autumn.

Occasionally the cover of primrose ripples and bubbles from the movement of large carp. Great Blue Heron and Great Egret spear for fish and frogs along the edges of the marsh. Also present are Black-crowned Night Heron and American Bittern. Most of these birds roost in the riparian forest and utilize the marsh as a feeding area.

A walk through the Valley Oak Woodland is most rewarding. From the tangled banks you emerge into an open understory dominated by Creeping Wildrye and Santa Barbara Sedge. The openness lends a park-like feeling to the place, even though the tree canopy is completely closed overhead. Oak leaves crunch underfoot. Crows caw and hawks cry in the distance. Stop and listen to the wind rustle through the trees. Perhaps John Sutter did all this on his travels here more than a hundred years ago. Thanks to the Conservancy, your great grandchildren will be able to do the same.

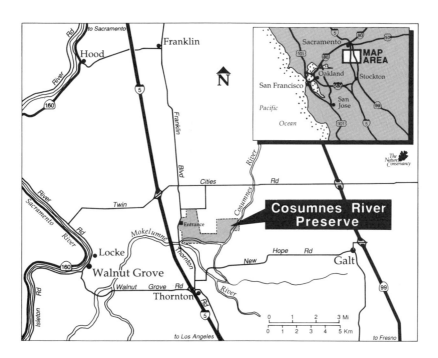

Cosumnes River Checklist

INFORMATION

For information contact the preserve manager at 7100 Desmond Road, Galt, CA 95632; (916) 686-6982.

SIZE

1,100 acres

SEASONAL HIGHLIGHTS

Sandhill Cranes, September through April; migratory waterfowl in fall; and marsh wildflower display, spring through July.

WEATHER

Mediterranean, with hot dry summers and cool, moist winters. Tule fogs are common midwinter.

ON-SITE FACILITIES

Self-guided nature trail

NEAREST OFF-SITE FACILITIES

22 miles north in Sacramento

EQUIPMENT

good walking shoes
binoculars
food and water

TIME REQUIRED

Half day

DIRECTIONS

Take the Twin Cities Road exit off Interstate 5 (from the south, 26 miles north of Stockton; from the north, 22 miles south of Sacramento). Follow Twin Cities Road east to Franklin Blvd. Turn right onto Franklin Blvd. and proceed south 1.5 miles to nature trail entrance.

Greater Sandhill Crane

Grus canadensis tabida

THE SANDHILL Crane is one of the oldest living species of birds in the world. Bones exactly like those of today's Sandhills have been found in Pliocene and Pleistocene deposits dating back four to nine million years. Before settlement times, Sandhills nested from the Atlantic seaboard to the Pacific Northwest, from Cuba to the Arctic. But loss of habitat has isolated them into six distinct subspecies. Largest in size is the Greater Sandhill Crane (*Grus canadensis tabida*); with a wingspan of six to seven feet when fully mature, it is bigger than a Great Blue Heron. The smallest is the Lesser Sandhill Crane (*Grus canadensis canadensis*). Both migrate south through California during late fall, then north again in spring. Many flocks winter in the Central Valley—you can spot them at the Carrizo Plain and Cosumnes River preserves. Greater Sandhills nest primarily in Oregon and Northern California, and Lesser Sandhills nest in the Arctic.

Like its more famous cousin the Whooping Crane, the Greater Sandhill is long-legged, long-necked, stately, and rare. Mouse-gray in color, it sports a bald red crown and a tuft over its tail that marks it as a crane. Juveniles are brownish and lack the crimson head. Greater Sandhills are easy to distinguish from Great Blue Herons in flight. The heron flies with its head drawn back and its neck in a loop, whereas the crane fully extends its neck. The crane's wing motion has a distinctive flick or flap above body level, too, and the heron's has a bowed downstroke.

Sandhills mate for life. Prior to nesting season, cranes perform a showy mating dance. The male hops up and down in front of the female until she enters the dance. Then they hop together—as high as twelve feet off the ground, stiff-legged and wings half outstretched. The dance can last from several seconds to several minutes.

Nests are built in marshy areas in spring and resemble mounds of hay. The female lays on average two eggs, which are usually spotted and olive

Sandhill Crane

in color. Fledglings start to fly at three months. Juvenile mortality, however, is high — Common Raven, Raccoon, and Coyote prey on both eggs and young.

Nesting success is especially vulnerable to human disturbance. Low-flying aircraft can flush incubating birds, exposing the eggs to avian predators. Roads, trails, and railroad tracks provide mammalian predators with more access to nesting grounds. And grazing by livestock reduces groundcover, making the nests easier to find.

NINE

Jepson Prairie

Beauty Blooms in Spring

WHEN SPEEDING along Interstate 80 or up and down Interstate 5, it's hard to imagine the view California's early settlers had 150 years ago. For them, the lush, manicured Central Valley was a sea of untamed prairie. And where a seamless patchwork of orderly crops and plowed fields now grows, colorful wildflowers and native bunchgrasses once covered the land.

Most of the state's original 23 million acres of grasslands fell under the harrow long ago—less than one percent is now in its natural condition—but 1,566 acres remain unplowed near Dixon, a sleepy farming community 76 miles east of San Francisco. An unusual relic of early California, these acres are the Jepson Prairie Preserve—a living laboratory for scientists, a refuge for five rare and endangered species, and a place of subtle beauty and quiet reflection.

The preserve is named for one of California's foremost botanists, Willis Linn Jepson. Jepson was born in nearby Vacaville in 1867 and conducted pioneer research on vernal pools where the preserve stands today. Fittingly, the preserve serves as a living classroom for students and professors from nearby UC Davis. The preserve is managed jointly by the Conservancy and the University of California Natural Land Reserves System.

Jepson Prairie's most striking feature is a collection of vernal pools, commonly referred to as "hog wallows." The pools are actually shallow depressions underlain by an impervious layer of clay where rainwater collects during winter months. They are rarely deeper than two feet. In spring, when the pools start to evaporate, wildflowers grow and bloom, creating concentric rings of white and yellow and blue around the shrinking body of water. By summer the water is gone, leaving behind dry, cracked soil. The fragile pools are unique ecosystems; more than three-fourths of their plants are native species.

Fritillaria liliacea

Jepson Prairie has one of the world's largest vernal pools. Called Olcott Pool, it is home to several rare and endangered species, including the California Tiger Salamander, a fairy shrimp, and Solano Grass, a plant that grows nowhere else on earth. The Delta Green Ground Beetle is another species whose last known population is here.

Southern Patwin Indians once foraged for food in and around Olcott Pool, while herds of Tule Elk, Pronghorn, and Grizzly Bears roamed in the waving fields of Purple Needlegrass and Melic Grass. Within the past century the area became surrounded by farms and pastures. Concern for its future led The Nature Conservancy to purchase the land from Southern Pacific Railroad in 1980. The preserve was formally dedicated in April 1982.

In early spring, fields of flowering Blennospermas, Downingias, four species of Goldfields, Popcorn Flowers, Star Lilies, and Johnny Jump-ups put on a colorful show. The blooms change almost weekly. One of the more interesting plants growing on the preserve is Meadowfoam. Seeds of related species contain a wax that is nearly identical to sperm whale oil. Botanists are looking into the possibility of producing the wax commercially as a replacement for the whale oil, which is valued as an industrial lubricant because it can withstand high temperatures.

◄ *Jepson Prairie Preserve*

The best way to visit Jepson Prairie is by joining one of the regularly scheduled docent-led trips. The docents share a wealth of information and can point out the finer details of the preserve. The guided walks follow a trail that passes trees busy with birds—juncos, towhees, Scrub Jays, Loggerhead Shrikes, flycatchers, and even Great Horned Owls are frequently spotted.

The trail leads down to Olcott Pool. Keep an eye out for nesting shorebirds and waterfowl that float in rafts out in the middle of the water. Jepson Prairie lies along the major flyway for such species as Mallard, American Wigeon, Northern Pintail, Common Merganser, and Canada Goose migrating south to sunnier climes.

As you circumnavigate the pool, walk out into the middle of the prairie and stop and look around. The scenery is spectacular in minute appointments. For those with patience, a special world awaits in the tussocks of bunchgrass.

One of the more unusual features you'll notice are strange-looking mounds of earth. These are called mima mounds. How they are created has given rise to several theories. The leading explanation is that burrowing animals formed the mounds by piling up soil when digging holes for their homes.

California grassland evolved under a combination of unchecked wildfires and native grazing animals. To evaluate the impact these factors have on floristics, researchers at Jepson Prairie Preserve are experimenting with controlled burning and grazing. Sheep—they are thought to better mimic the foraging habits of Pronghorn and Tule Elk than cattle—have been pastured in certain areas; other locations are burned periodically, and some areas are left untouched.

To the casual eye, Jepson Prairie's landscape appears unassuming, but the preserve is very much alive with wildlife. As field mice scamper between tufts of Purple Needlegrass, Red-tailed Hawks soar overhead in pursuit. Swarms of Red-winged Blackbirds swirl like storm clouds on the horizon. The deep honk of Canada Geese provides contrapuntal harmony to the melodic song of Western Meadowlarks. As the grass undulates in the breeze, listen to the hiss of the wind as it rushes by. It all conjures up a passage from Willa Cather's *My Antonia*:

I felt motion in the landscape; in the fresh, easy-blowing morning wind, and in the earth itself, as if the shaggy grass were sort of a loose hide, and underneath it herds of wild buffalo were galloping, galloping . . .

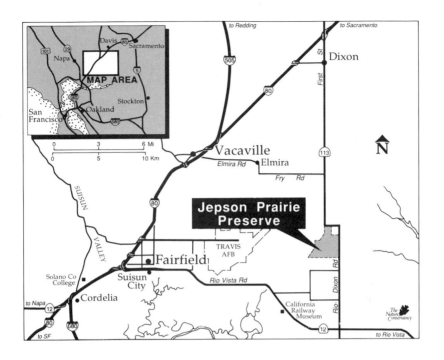

Jepson Prairie Checklist

Visitation is by docent-led tours only. They are held on weekends 10 A.M. to 12 P.M. from mid-February to the end of flowering season, usually mid-May. For reservations or access permission, contact the Institute of Ecology, University of California, Davis, CA 95616; (916) 752-6580.

SIZE

1,566 acres

SEASONAL HIGHLIGHTS

Spring wildflowers, early February through May; waterfowl in February and March.

WEATHER

Windy. Cool in early spring. Hot afternoons in May.

ON–SITE FACILITIES

None

NEAREST OFF–SITE FACILITIES

14 miles north in town of Dixon

EQUIPMENT

good walking shoes
binoculars
food and water

TIME REQUIRED

2 to 3 hours

DIRECTIONS

Jepson Prairie is about a 1½ hour drive east of San Francisco via Interstate 80. From I 80, take Highway 113 south through Dixon. Continue south on 113 for 14 miles straight onto Cook Lane when 113 doglegs left at the yellow flashing lights. Continue on the dirt road for three-quarters of a mile and park on the shoulder. There is a sign marking the entrance to the preserve.

Delta Green Ground Beetle

Elaphrus viridis

L OST FOR nearly a century, the Delta Green Ground Beetle was rediscovered in 1974 by a UC Davis student searching for bugs in the Jepson Prairie area. Prior to that, the last confirmed sighting of this brilliant, metallic green insect was made in 1878 by pioneer entomologist George H. Horn.

The Delta Green is oblong and measures roughly one-third of an inch long — about the size and shape of a pinky fingernail. It has moderately large eyes and somewhat resembles the more common tiger beetle. But the ground beetle's active movements and extreme reluctance to fly makes it easily distinguishable.

The beetle inhabits the grassland associated with vernal pools and is not known to occur anywhere else in the world outside of the Jepson Prairie environs. Because its habitat is so limited, it has been added to the federal list of threatened species of wildlife.

Delta Greens are most frequently sighted between February and May. Diurnal, they become active on sunny, nonwindy days when the temperature is between 62 and 70 degrees. Heat or cold renders them less mobile; they are more apt to spend their time underneath vegetation obscured from view. The same holds true during windy days. Beetles can lose their grip when gusts exceed twenty miles per hour and get blown across the fields.

Delta Greens are predators and rely on soft-bodied insects for food. The bulk of their diet is composed of springtails — a light tan insect smaller than a hyphen. The beetle uses three methods for hunting. In open-area hunting, it wanders over sandy areas between patches of vegetation and chases any prey that moves. The second technique centers on "feeding arenas," small, circular openings in the vegetation. The beetle enters the arena, waits for unwary springtails to wander in, then attacks. The springtail has a hard time hopping over the surrounding

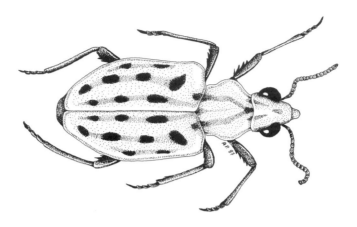

Delta Green Ground Beetle

vegetation, which serves as a fence. Finally, the beetle hunts in cavities, vertical holes in sandy mud that act as natural springtail pitfall traps.

In turn, the beetle is prey for the Pacific Treefrog, another highly camouflaged, ambush predator of the vernal pools. Shorebirds probably have little effect on the beetle, since it freezes when it detects the movement of larger objects and is almost impossible to see when motionless.

Agriculture, however, has had a major effect. Conversion and subsequent plowing represent a permanent loss of habitat, and grazing poses problems as well. Turning Jepson Prairie into a permanent preserve has helped keep the Delta Green from extinction.

T E N

Elkhorn Slough

Of Mice and Marsh

YOU DON'T have to journey all the way to a tropical rain forest to find a place brimming with different species of wildlife. Elkhorn Slough, a coastal wetland located at the northern tip of Steinbeck country midway between Santa Cruz and Monterey, is home to hundreds of species of marine invertebrates, eighty types of fishes, and is used by nearly three hundred species of birds.

Estuaries, areas where fresh water meets salt water, are among the most productive habitats in the biological world, but they are also among the most endangered. In California, for instance, nearly ninety percent have been destroyed. Fortunately, the Elkhorn Slough estuary, the state's largest estuarine system after San Francisco Bay, is being saved and remains a vital breeding and feeding ground for wildlife. It owes its survival in part to The Nature Conservancy and state and federal agencies.

Elkhorn Slough occupies an ancient seven-mile-long river channel that winds through a peaceful valley planted with fields of brussels sprouts and strawberries. Along its edge are more than 2,500 acres of submerged and semi-submerged lands. This luscious belt of mudflats and marsh is banked by thickets bright with yellow flowering field mustard, Red-stem Filaree, Blue Dicks, and lupine. Coast Live Oak and eucalyptus groves grow on the surrounding marine terraces. Tens of thousands of shorebirds winter here, not to mention countless flocks of passing waterfowl that touch down in migration. Their chatter and call fill the air in fall and again in spring.

At one time Elkhorn Slough shared a common mouth with the Salinas River, but in 1908 the river was diverted, and the slough became a tidal embayment opening into Monterey Bay. The estuary is seasonal with freshwater runoff occurring only in rainy months. During summer months, evaporation causes the water to become hypersaline. A unique

community of plants in the slough has adapted to these fluctuating conditions and is able to withstand inundation by sea water.

The most dominant plant in the salt marsh is Pickleweed, a succulent able to retain enough water within its tissues to withstand flooding by salty ocean waters. The stages of its growth are tied to the seasons, and seasonally it turns different colors, from pale green in spring and summer to crimson in fall. Pickleweed flanks hundreds of acres of mudflat and channel, providing food and cover for many animals — five of which are listed as rare and endangered.

A shy brown bird known as the California Clapper Rail is one of the slough's rarest creatures. It nests in the higher reaches of the salt marsh and rarely ventures far from the Pickleweed. Another endangered bird is the California Brown Pelican. The salt ponds near the slough's mouth are the bird's most important summer roosting grounds north of Point Conception. Santa Cruz Long-toed Salamanders inhabit several of the freshwater ponds, and the rare brackish water snail, *Tryonia imitator*, can be found in quieter waters. The endangered Salinas Harvest Mouse is thought to depend on the marsh for survival. And the Peregrine Falcon haunts the slough on a seasonal basis.

The tidally bathed mudflats support a tremendous number of invertebrates. Most of the mudflat residents are hidden from view, but scientific measurements show as many as 100,000 organisms living within a square meter at the surface. As the tide recedes, life on the mudflats is revealed. Tiny sand fleas scurry across the surface, while small crabs spring out of their holes to gather food. There are 28 species of clams living in the mud, not to mention numerous species of oysters, crabs, and amphipods.

With tidal movement, abundant food is washed into the slough's open water. Elkhorn Slough is also a vital nursery and feeding area for many commercial species of fish and shellfish. The slough flushes into the Monterey Bay Submarine Canyon — a cavity deeper than the Grand Canyon and considered to be an important resource to the Pacific Coast fishing industry. Salmon, albacore, anchovy, rock fish, herring, and sole are just a few of the species that dwell there.

The fecundity of the estuary has supported humans for millennia. Coastanoan (also known as Ohlone) Indians established villages by the slough 5,000 years ago. They hunted Tule Elk and duck and gathered shellfish. Their shell middens scattered along the shore still remain. Archaeologists recently uncovered a village site at the mouth of Elkhorn Slough only twenty feet from Highway 1. The dig yielded several human skeletons buried ten feet below the soil surface. One man was still wearing long strands of beads fashioned from over 3,000 olive

◄ *Elkhorn Slough Preserve*

shells, a common snail in the lower slough. Bones of Sea Otters, Harbor Seals, and seabirds were also found.

American settlers discovered the valley in the 1800s and built homes and farms in the surrounding uplands. Eventually they diked and filled large areas of the marsh to make more farmland. Hudson's Landing was established at the head of the slough. This small port was used by local farmers to transport grain downstream to Moss Landing, a picturesque fishing town, where it was loaded onto coastal schooners bound for San Francisco. The history of coastal shipping here was brief, however. In the 1870s, the Southern Pacific Railroad brought rail service to the area — the tracks were laid right along the edge of the slough.

World War II introduced the first heavy industry to Elkhorn Slough. Kaiser built a refractory plant in 1942, and in 1952, Pacific Gas and Electric constructed a large steam electric generating plant near the mouth. Commercial salt ponds were also created as companies diked portions of the slough for mineral extraction.

Concern for Elkhorn Slough's future led The Nature Conservancy to begin negotiating for property in 1968. In 1971 and 1972, the Conservancy was able to set aside 180 acres at the upper end of the slough. Two years later it added 163 acres of prime marshland. In the years that followed, the Conservancy protected additional acreage through conservation easements or outright property purchase. In 1984, it assisted the California Wildlife Conservation Board in acquiring 554 acres of salt ponds and marshes at the mouth of the slough.

Elkhorn Slough Preserve now totals 388 acres. Three rare communities are represented: Northern Eusaline Lagoon, Northern Coastal Saltmarsh, and Coastal Freshwater Marsh. You can walk from groves of Coast Live Oak in the uplands down to the water at the edge of the marsh.

The oaks provide perching areas to resident and migratory birds. The acorns are an important food source, and cavities in the dead or partially decayed limbs and trunks are used as nests and denning areas by Northern Flickers, Downy Woodpeckers, Plain Titmice, Gray Foxes, and Raccoons. Hawks and owls roost in the taller trees.

Down at water's edge yet another avian community exists. Sandpipers, dowitchers, Willets, Avocets, Marbled Godwits, and herons search for food in the mudflats, while Coots, Pintails, teal, Shovelers, and Western Grebes feed in the open water.

The preserve is adjacent to the 1,300-acre Elkhorn Slough National Estuarine Research Reserve. One of seventeen such reserves established nationwide, it is managed by the California Department of Fish and Game under an agreement with the Division of Marine and Estuarine Management of the National Oceanic and Atmospheric Administration. The Reserve not only helps to protect this vital habitat for wetland-dependent life, but also ensures that scientists and the general public can

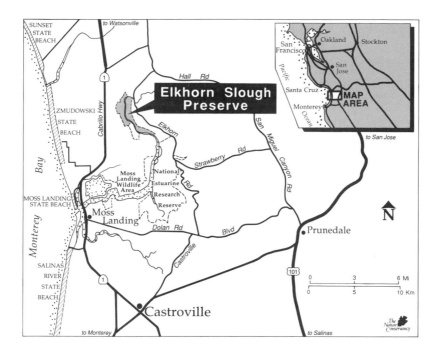

learn about coastal and estuarine ecology in a natural setting. It is the perfect complement to The Nature Conservancy preserve, and the two programs have worked side by side.

In fact, programs on both properties are coordinated by the Elkhorn Slough Foundation, a nonprofit organization founded to help further education and research programs and promote preservation of the Elkhorn Slough ecosystem.

The Elkhorn Slough interpretive guides, who volunteer for both the Conservancy preserve and the Estuarine Reserve, staff the Reserve Visitor Center, a gray brick building trimmed in cerulean blue and festooned with colorful banners. Inside are maps, guides, and interpretive galleries. A naturalist is on hand to answer questions.

There are five miles of trails at Elkhorn Slough Reserve. South Marsh Loop leads you through fields of wildflowers down to the marsh. First stop is the site of the abandoned Elkhorn Dairy, where you can poke among old farming relics outside a weather-beaten barn that overlooks the ancient river valley. The trail continues down an embankment to a salt marsh edged with red-tipped Pickleweed and several other colorful succulents. Eventually the trail doglegs left down to the slough's main channel.

Together, the National Estuarine Reserve and the Elkhorn Slough Preserve, along with the California Department of Fish and Game and the

Department of Parks and Recreation, are helping to protect this unique and important coastal habitat.

Elkhorn Slough Checklist

INFORMATION

The National Estuarine Research Reserve entrance to Elkhorn Slough is open Thursday through Sunday, 9 A.M. to 5 P.M. Guided tours at the Reserve are scheduled. For more information, contact the Elkhorn Slough Foundation, P.O. Box 267, Moss Landing, CA 95039; or the Reserve Visitor Center at (408) 728-2822. The Nature Conservancy offers guided tours of its specially designated private preserve. For more information, call (408) 728-2822.

SIZE

388 acres

SEASONAL HIGHLIGHTS

Summer brings California Brown Pelicans; bird migrations in fall; winter is good birding.

WEATHER

Varied coastal climate: relatively mild, wet, cool winters and cool, dry summers. Frequent fog in spring and summer.

ON-SITE FACILITIES

Visitor Center on the adjacent National Estuarine Research Reserve; hiking trails, volunteer-led walks.

NEAREST OFF-SITE FACILITIES

Moss Landing is at the mouth of the slough with restaurants, harbor facilities, and shops.

EQUIPMENT

good walking shoes
binoculars
food and water

TIME REQUIRED

Half day

DIRECTIONS

Elkhorn Slough is about a 2½ hour drive from San Francisco. Taking Highway 1 south, turn left on Dolan Road just before Moss Landing and go 3½ miles to Elkhorn Road. Turn left and go another 2½ miles until you reach the Visitor Center located on the lefthand side of the road. It's clearly marked.

ELEVEN

Landels-Hill Big Creek

Semper Fidelis to Sempervirens

A LONG CALIFORNIA's entire 1100-mile coastline, no wild place is more dramatic, more storied than Big Sur. The never-ending song of the Pacific pounding on black rock beaches and the striking beauty of seawind-sculpted headlands inspires the senses as well as the soul.

Big Sur is sheer poetry. Robinson Jeffers' images are everywhere, and nowhere more so than at Big Creek. Here, near-vertical cliffs rise dramatically from the cobbled shore. A clean, clear stream pushes its way through boulders in a canyon cloaked by redwoods and lush with sorrel and ferns. Higher still, fast-moving fog scrapes the tops of wind-sheared oaks and bays, ruffles the blades in open fields of grass. Flocks of Song Sparrows rattle the tips of dry chaparral. A Mountain Lion screams.

Forty-five miles south of Carmel, Big Creek lies in the heart of the Santa Lucia Mountains. Nowhere else in the contiguous states do mountains rise so abruptly from the ocean. Cone Peak, from which Big Creek drains, climbs 5,155 feet in little more than three miles. The dramatic difference in climate between the peak's summit and sea level makes for an incredible number of spatially compressed habitat zones. As a result, 23 distinct plant communities coincide at Big Creek, encompassing some 479 different species of vascular plants and 21 moss and liverwort species. Eight are listed by the California Native Plant Society as either rare or endangered.

The floral diversity is also affected by the mixing of two floristic elements; Big Creek straddles the cool Oregon Province and the more temperate California Province. Plants usually associated with the moist coastal forests of the north mingle with those more typical of dry southern regions. Imagine: Yucca growing side by side with Coast Redwood.

Big Creek also harbors many relict and endemic species as well as several disjunct ones. The rugged topography of the Santa Lucia Mountains

Landels-Hill Big Creek Preserve

has created an "island effect," an isolation that has led to speciation. Santa Lucia Fir and Hoover's Manzanita are just two of the resultant endemics. Four species, usually limited to either the Cascade or Sierra Nevada ranges, have also found their way to Big Creek: Ponderosa Pine, Sugar Pine, Phantom Orchid, and Spotted Coral-root.

No wonder that botanists have been coming to Big Creek for more than a century. Thomas Coulter, Alice Eastwood, and Willis Linn Jepson are among the scientific luminaries who have spent time here helping to shed light on this strange juxtaposition of plant associations.

The vegetation supports a wide range of animals as well. Fifteen species of reptiles and five species of amphibians occur here. More than 125 species of birds have been identified, including Spotted Owl, Goshawk, Peregrine Falcon, and Golden Eagle. The site's 51 species of mammals range in size from the tiny White-footed Deer Mouse to Black-tailed Mule Deer. Bobcats are common. You can spot their scratch marks on the roads and trails.

In recognition of Big Creek's important ecological significance, several landowners in the area agreed to sell their property to The Nature

Conservancy in 1977. The bulk of the site was subsequently transferred to the University of California to become part of the university's Natural Land Reserve System. The university holds title to more than 3,800 acres; 40 acres remain in Conservancy ownership. The reserve provides students, professors, field scientists, and nature lovers with a unique opportunity to study and explore nearly 3,840 acres of relatively undisturbed wildland, including some three miles of coast.

Like the terrestrial habitats, the shoreline contains elements of both the Oregon and California provinces. Narrow and discontinuous, the intertidal shelf is exposed to wave stress, an extreme physical hardship for its inhabitants.

Marine life is unusual. Two rare creatures, the California Sea Otter, a subtidal keystone species, and the Owl Limpet, an intertidal keystone species, have coexisted since Pleistocene times. Diversity is also great. Eighty-eight species of intertidal algae have been identified, including two that represent the most southerly extension of their range. There are 192 species of intertidal invertebrates. Six of them are at the limit of their ranges. Of the 38 species of shore birds and seabirds, one, the California Brown Pelican, is federally listed as endangered. From January through April, Orca and migrating Gray Whale can be seen from shore.

The best way to explore Landels-Hill Big Creek is to take the interpretive trail on a Conservancy field trip. The four-mile loop is somewhat strenuous with a climb and descent of more than a thousand feet, but it offers a representative view of the site's natural features. What's more, it provides entry to the poetic marvel that is Big Sur.

The trail begins from the parking lot near the reserve's entrance. Follow the road to the confluence of Big Creek and Devil's Creek. The road was built around 1930 shortly after Highway 1 was completed. Before that time, much of Big Sur was accessible only on foot or horseback. Lack of roads kept the area from being settled, except for the handful of homesteaders who built small cabins and lived off the land. Prior to that, Big Creek was home to two tribes of native Americans, the Esselens and the Salinians.

Little is known about the Esselens. They were a small tribe numbering about 1,000 at the time of the first European contact in 1769. Within a century, they had disappeared from the Big Sur coast: Spanish padres enticed them to move to the missions of the Salinas Valley and Monterey Peninsula. Disease and forced labor led to their decline. Anthropologists believe they were the first California Indian group to have become extinct.

The first thing you'll notice as you begin the hike is that the area was severely burned. On July 6, 1985, a lightning storm struck an oak tree on a ridge overlooking Big Creek, touching off a 57,000-acre blaze that raged for two weeks. The fire burned through the entire preserve, scorching all 23 vegetation types. Though devastating, it was not unusual.

Fire occurs regularly in the coastal mountains—at least seven major fires swept through Big Creek between 1900 and 1941.

Most of the vegetation has adapted to cope with fire. Coast Redwood, California Bay, and Tanbark Oak, for instance, have all developed thick burls at the base of their trunks and insulating bark to protect their cores from flames. Other trees produce seeds or cones that germinate best after a fire. Just two years after the 1985 blaze, Big Creek was already well on its way to healing itself.

A footbridge takes you over Devil's Creek above its confluence with Big Creek. Together, these two streams drain nearly 24 square miles of the Santa Lucia Mountains. Even in drought years, they never run dry. That Big Creek can support one of the southernmost runs of steelhead in the state attests to the ecological health and purity of the area. The creek's water is clean enough to drink. This area has been designated as the California Coast Range Biosphere Reserve by UNESCO.

Heading upstream, the trail passes beneath a towering canopy of redwoods that shade a natural fern grotto made up of Venus-hair, Maidenhair, Five-finger, Sword, and Bracken ferns. Flowering Honeysuckle, California Blackberry, Huckleberry, Wood Rose, and Star Flower add a delicate beauty to the understory. Beyond, the forest opens. Here, several shrub species become more common: Sticky Monkeyflower, Creambush, and Thimbleberry. John Muir's favorite bird, the Dipper, bobs on the rocks in the middle of the creek. Brown Creeper clings to the side of trees, and Dark-eyed Junco and Hermit Thrush call from the limbs.

The trail leaves Big Creek and follows one of its tributaries, Brunnette Creek, named for Rooth Brunnette who built a cabin along the creek's banks in the early 1930s. All that remains of the cabin today are a few charred posts. It is one of several historic homesteads in the area destroyed by the 1985 blaze.

As the trail climbs above the creek, redwoods are replaced by Coast Live Oaks and other hardwoods. The terrain turns drier, and vegetation abruptly changes. Ceanothus, California Coffeeberry, and Coyote Brush now dominate the landscape. The shrubbery opens to a rocky overlook where three vegetation types meet: Mixed Hardwood Forest, Coastal Sage Scrub, and Open Grassland.

From here you can look across the canyon at the vegetation on the opposite hillsides. The different plant communities have turned the natural landscape into a beautiful mosaic. On one hillside, an open field of Wild Oat, Blue-eyed Grass, and Purple Needlegrass lies between a band of Ceanothus shrubs and Coastal Sage Scrub. Above this is a forest of Coast Live Oak, Madrone, and California Bay. Western Fence Lizards sun themselves on the nearby rocks. Soaring over the canyons are Red-tailed Hawks and Turkey Vultures. White-throated Swifts and Violet-green Swallows swoop low over the open faces of the hillsides.

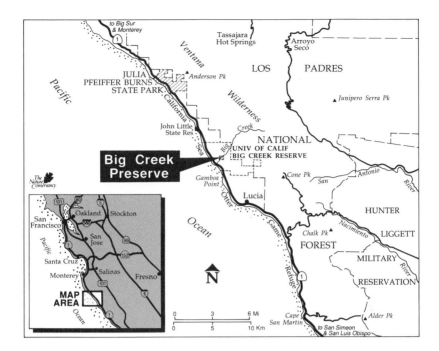

From here you can see all the way from the ocean to the top of Cone Peak. It is a breathtaking sight. As hawks screech and the wind blows, these words of Jeffers come to mind, "here where enormous sundowns/ flower and burn through color to quietness":

. . . the greatest beauty is/organic wholeness, the wholeness of life and things, the divine/beauty of the universe. Love that, not man/apart from that . . .

Landels-Hill Big Creek Checklist

INFORMATION

Access to the preserve is by Conservancy field trips only. For more information, contact the Conservancy at 785 Market Street, San Francisco, CA 94103; (415) 777-0487.

SIZE

3,848 acres, 40 of which remain in Conservancy ownership; the remainder has been transferred to the University of California.

SEASONAL HIGHLIGHTS

Wildflower display in spring; whale watching January through April.

WEATHER

Coastal maritime climate, with cool, foggy summers and mild, rainy winters.

ON-SITE FACILITIES

Interpretive trail; outhouse

NEAREST OFF-SITE FACILITIES

15 miles north in Big Sur

EQUIPMENT

good walking shoes
binoculars
food and water
sun protection
Poison-oak protection

TIME REQUIRED

3 to 4 hours

DIRECTIONS

The preserve is located 45 miles south of Carmel on Highway 1. Turn east into the entrance at the south end of Big Creek Bridge. Park in the designated parking lot.

TWELVE

Kaweah Oaks

Beneath the Old Oak Tree

THE OAK tree is to California what the skyscraper is to Manhattan, the wheat field to Kansas. No other species better symbolizes the state. Picture California and more often than not the scene includes an oak. But these trees do much more than enhance the landscape. They have long provided for the natural economy. Not only do oaks supply food and shelter for countless animals, but prior to European settlement, the acorn harvest helped feed the West's densest concentration of Indians. Pioneers settled among the oaks, realizing that the big trees took root in the best agricultural soils. The trees shaded them from the sun, heated their houses, fired their machines, and supplied them with the raw materials to manufacture the tools of frontier life. From Oakland to Thousand Oaks, and dozens of places between, the names of California towns honor the old oak trees.

Sadly, those place names are often the only reminder that lush groves of oaks once grew where subdivisions and shopping centers now stand. Nearly all of California's fifteen species of oaks are being seriously challenged. The stately, deciduous Valley Oak is under intense pressure.

The Valley Oak is among the largest oaks found anywhere in the world. It grows rapidly and can reach truly impressive size—trees 12 feet in diameter and 150 feet tall are not uncommon. Valley Oaks are also long-lived. Many of the largest trees standing today were around when Don Gaspar de Portola first explored California back in 1769.

The Valley Oak normally grows in open groves on well-watered soil that is relatively deep and fertile. Because the trees can root deeply and quickly—seedlings root down almost three feet in the few wet winter months following natural germination—Valley Oak have adapted to withstand drought conditions that wither most other plants.

Originally, Valley Oaks stretched from the Sacramento River and Pit River canyons in the north to the San Fernando Valley, 500 miles south.

Valley Oak

The densest groves crowded the rivers of California's Great Central Valley. The largest concentration occurred on the delta of the Kaweah River. There, more than 400 square miles of Valley Oak flourished.

Valley Oak Woodland began to disappear in the 1850s when the state's population boomed and fields and forests were converted into farms and orchards. Because it was the only source of wood in an otherwise treeless land, Valley Oak was cut for fuel and fenceposts. Square mile after square mile was cut and shipped to San Francisco, where the wood heated houses until this century.

Only a fraction of the original Valley Oak Woodland remains. One of the best and largest remnants is found on a 324-acre parcel located six miles east of Visalia. Purchased in 1983 by The Nature Conservancy to be protected as a permanent preserve, Kaweah Oaks lies on the floodplain of the Kaweah River. The river drains Sequoia National Park, and one of its distributaries, Deep Creek, flows through the preserve. Two manmade canals, Davis Ditch and People's Ditch, also traverse the site. People's Ditch, built over a century ago, was the first community-sponsored irrigation project in the state.

The waterways are lined with magnificent stands of 50- to 150-year-old Valley Oaks as well as Western Sycamore, Fremont Cottonwood, Oregon Ash, and four species of willow. Beneath the towering trees grows a lush understory of Elderberry, California Blackberry, Wild Grape, and Wild Rye Grass.

◄ *Kaweah Oaks Preserve*

The understory today seems thick enough, but it is not nearly as dense as it was around the turn of the century. The site was used for pasture for over a century, and decades of cattle grazing, in addition to the many fires set in the 1920s and 1930s, have taken their toll on the groundcover and oak saplings. As a result, several species of alien plants have become established. Patches of Himalayan Blackberry quickly outcompeted the native variety, their thorns giving them the advantage when it came to defending against hungry cattle. Milk Thistle and Poison Hemlock—two naturalized Europeans—were also introduced.

The Conservancy is currently hard at work eliminating these exotics, and cows have been excluded from much of the woodland for several years now. Already the effect is noticeable. California Blackberry is reclaiming some of its former territory, while California Wild Rose, now protected from trampling by hooves, has also returned. Efforts are underway to rid the site of the aggressive thistle and hemlock invaders.

Visalia's first settlers referred to Kaweah Oaks as a "jungle" and a "swamp." The abundant groundwater fosters prolific growth throughout warm summers, producing luxuriant vegetation. Wild Grape growing in thick lianas up to 70 feet long dangle from the spreading limbs of the oak trees. Back in the golden age of Hollywood, they were used on the set of Tarzan movies. Studios paid a penny a foot for the vines, and more than one valley kid made a summer job out of helping Johnny Weismuller swing.

The grapes also supply fruit for many birds and other animals, and were once food for Grizzly Bears and resident Yokuts Indians.

Another vine creeping through the woodland is Clematis, also known as Virgin's Bower. This native tends to grow horizontally, overgrowing other low ground cover, and its leafy growth provides excellent shelter for small mammals and birds trying to avoid Red-shouldered, Sharp-shinned, and Cooper's hawks hunting overhead.

The woodland supports a diverse array of animal life. Over 125 species of birds use this important natural area, as do 11 species of reptiles and amphibians (including the California Legless Lizard), and 14 species of mammals.

Keep a look out on the tree trunks and you'll likely see different species of breeding woodpecker: Northern Flicker, and Downy, Nuttall's, and Acorn woodpeckers. Red-breasted Sapsuckers have also been sighted here. The woodpeckers chip cavities in the trees which, in turn, create places for nine other species of birds to nest in, including House Wren, Tree Swallow, Ash-throated Flycatcher, and Plain Titmouse. Other nesters at the preserve are the Black-headed Grosbeak, Blue Grosbeak, Lazuli Bunting, and Northern Oriole.

The air is filled with birdsong, especially during the peak of the spring and fall migrations. Solitary Vireo and Warbling Vireo wheeze, whistle,

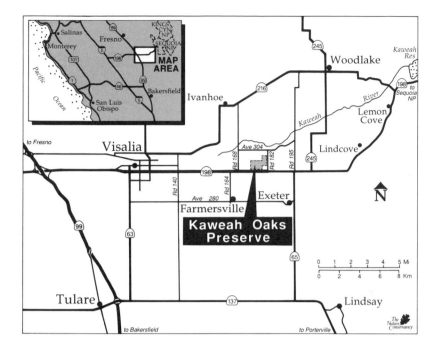

and buzz from the limbs, while seven different types of warblers, including Orange-crowned, Yellow-rumped, and Black-throated Gray warblers, lend a dash of contrast to the brown and green backdrop.

The preserve is about 45 percent clothed in woods. The remainder is divided between streambed, open field, and meadow. There are also several ponds on the property. Turtle Pond, named for the large number of Western Pond Turtles living there, is actually an oxbow. It is a nesting site for the colorful Wood Duck, along with Great Blue Heron and Mallard. Garter Snakes can be found slithering around its banks.

In the middle of the preserve, near the entrance, is a large meadow that supports a very different community of flora compared to the bottomland near the creeks. Salt Grass, Sticky Sand-spurrey, Clustered Field Sedge, Alkali Sacaton, and Cone Flower are the most prevalent plants growing here. The meadow is the result of topography that places it higher and drier than surrounding areas.

The preserve has a high water table, about seven to ten feet deep under the meadow and closer to the surface nearer the water courses. Water moves upward through the soil for most of the year. During the late spring, summer, and fall, the soil water evaporates off the soil surface, leaving behind a layer of salt that accumulates. Where the concentrations of salt are highest, the soil is frosted white. Because the meadow area does not flood as often as the woodland, salt accumulations in the surface soil have resulted in very different levels of nutrients, salts, and species of plants.

All soil at Kaweah Oaks is of alluvial origin. Grading of the soil particle sizes from the streambeds upslope to the meadow is especially obvious: the streambeds and levees along them are sand, whereas the terraces along the creeks are silt, and the meadows silty loam.

At the north edge of the meadow lies a tract of land nicknamed "The North Forty." This relatively undisturbed patch of woodland is watched over by a huge Western Sycamore. Near the top of the tree is a gigantic nest. In spring, if you're lucky, you might be able to see a pair of Red-tailed Hawk fledglings peering over the side.

Leaves crunch and Wild Rye rasps in the wind as you walk beneath the intertwining arms of oaks, willows, and sycamores. On the ground grow vines of Coyote Melon. Centuries ago Yokuts children played a kind of soccer with these softball-sized gourds. During hard times, they were used for food. Western Fence Lizards race along the downed trunks of trees. Quail whoop from the underbrush, while California Ground Squirrels whistle their shrill alarm. Framed against the sky are the magnificent Valley Oaks, the picture of patience, endurance, and strength.

Kaweah Oaks Checklist

INFORMATION

For information contact the preserve manager at P.O. Box 3840, Visalia, CA 93278; (209) 627-4328.

SIZE

324 acres

SEASONAL HIGHLIGHTS

Wildflower display and bird migration in spring.

WEATHER

Mediterranean climate: long, hot, dry summers; short, cool, moist winters. Maximum temperature in summer often above 100 degrees, down to 38 degrees in winter. Frequent tule fog in winter. Average annual rainfall is 11 inches.

ON-SITE FACILITIES

Information kiosk, picnic tables, self-guided nature trails, and drinking fountain

NEAREST OFF-SITE FACILITIES

7 miles west in Visalia

EQUIPMENT

good walking shoes
binoculars
food and water

TIME REQUIRED

Half day

DIRECTIONS

Kaweah Oaks Preserve is located seven miles east of Visalia on the north side of Highway 198. Turn north on Road 182 and drive one-half mile to the preserve gate.

THIRTEEN

Creighton Ranch

A Natural Mosaic

ROM THE window seat of an airplane, the Central
Valley suggests a giant patchwork quilt. Mecha-
nized agriculture has stitched together geometrical shapes of green,
gold, and brown squares that cover the natural contour of the land and
turned the broad, meandering streams into straight and narrow seams.

How different it looks from 150 years ago. An aerial view back then
would have shown a rich mosaic of diversified habitats. Shallow lakes
the size of inland seas then splashed between the Sierra Nevada and
coastal ranges. Capable of expanding and contracting by miles (not feet)
in a single year, these lakes supported vast reaches of overflow marshland. A broad prairie of alkali scrub and grassland dotted by multihued
vernal pools spread over the valley floor. Below the foothills, thick
stands of Valley Oak studded the flatlands, and dense willow and cottonwood forests lined the riverbanks.

Little remains today of that natural tapestry. The giant lakes have all
been drained and most of the great rivers tamed. Of the valley's original
four million acres of wetland—far and away the greatest concentration
in all of California—over ninety-six percent has been destroyed. No
more than a handful of riparian woodland areas survive, and most of the
grassland savannah fell to the hungry harrow long ago.

Creighton Ranch is the only place left in the entire San Joaquin Valley
where all those pieces of the past still coincide. This 3,280-acre preserve
is located at the west end of Tulare County near the town of Corcoran.

Here, Coyotes still cross open fields of Mesquite as colorful bouquets
of Bird's-eye Gilia, Goldfields, and Blue Dicks bloom among the grassland. Stately Valley Oaks spread their branches over riverbanks. Flocks
of Black-crowned Night Herons roost in fragrant Buttonbush, while
ducks by the tens of thousands touch down on open ponds in the tule
marshes.

Eight plant communities listed as endangered by the California Natural Diversity Data Base grow on the preserve: Valley Iodine Bush Scrub, Valley Mesquite Scrub, Valley Seep-weed Scrub, Alkali Bunchgrass, Heavy Soil Flower Field, Northern Claypan Vernal Pool, Cattail Marsh, and Great Valley Mixed Riparian Forest.

This incredibly diverse melange of vegetation types supports an abundance of animal species unparalleled anywhere in the San Joaquin Valley. More than 220 species of birds have been sighted here, including such rarities as Horned Grebe, Bald Eagle, Sage Thrasher, Black-throated Blue Warbler, and Lark Bunting.

The preserve gets its name from Thomas Creighton, a homesteader who established a cattle ranch on the property in 1876. Prior to that, Tache Yokuts Indians lived here, no doubt attracted by the abundant waterfowl in the tule marshes and by the acorns, which they collected from the nearby riparian oak woodland and ground into meal.

Creighton built his ranch on the shore of Tulare Lake. At that time, the broad body of water was bigger than Lake Tahoe, stretching from Corcoran all the way across the valley to Kettleman City. The lake was so big, in fact, that the easiest way to get around it was by steamboat. Creighton Ranch served as a principal landing area for a 150-foot draught steamer christened the *Mose Androos*. This shallow boat carried people, hogs, and cattle to and from the tiny settlements that bordered the old lake. Steamboat service was short-lived, however. By the turn of the century the lake was drying up, a casualty of irrigated agriculture that usurped the water to convert wildland into farmland.

In the decades that followed, Creighton Ranch changed hands several times until 1956 when the nation's largest cotton producer, the J. G. Boswell Company, acquired the property. Recognizing the Ranch's outstanding ecological significance, it leased the site to The Nature Conservancy in 1980 to be managed as a nature preserve.

For more than a century the property was ranched, and the site's natural landscape underwent several significant alterations. To control flooding, the Tule River, which flows right through the middle of the preserve, was channelized. Canals were dug and a system of levees built. These produced Big Reservoir and Little Reservoir, two marshes totalling 900 acres that are used for water storage, reregulation, and control.

The levees provide visitors with an opportunity to view the marshes. Spring is an excellent time of year to visit. You can see wildflower displays, vernal pools, and such breeding songbirds as the Marsh Wren and Blue Grosbeak. During the peak of the fall waterfowl migration, the Ranch is a major stopping point along the great Pacific Flyway.

Begin at the interpretive center near the preserve's entrance. Pick up

◄ *Creighton Ranch Preserve*

a brochure and a map and orient yourself to the preserve's principal features. The interpretive displays help explain the natural history of the area, and thoughtfully conceived educational aids, such as the picture gallery of resident and migrant birds, give you a hint of what is in the field.

A self-guided, half-mile-long nature trail starts right outside the front door. It loops through three of the preserve's major plant communities: Alkali Scrub, Riparian Woodland, and Freshwater Marsh.

The Alkali Scrub community is testament to the size of old Tulare Lake. Its waters once covered portions of the preserve. As the lake ebbed and flowed, minerals accumulated in the soil that now supports patches of Salt Grass and Iodine Bush. Small vernal pools also dot the scrubland. Altogether, forty pools can be found on the preserve; most are short-lived except in very wet years.

The nature trail crosses an area that is seldom subject to flooding and therefore supports a great number of rodents and reptiles. They, in turn, attract numerous raptors. Desert Cottontails hop through the scrub under the watchful eyes of patrolling Red-tailed Hawks.

Eventually, the trail skirts the Tule River. Black Willow, Sandbar Willow, and Buttonbush crowd the banks. This riparian forest is a remnant; biologists estimate it to be a tenth of what it was prior to the 1920s. Nevertheless, the willow forest provides cover for a variety of bird species, including Black-headed Grosbeak, House Wren, and Bushtit. Other species to look for are Gray, Western, Olive-sided, Hammond's, and Dusky flycatchers as well as Nashville, Townsend's, MacGillivray's, Wilson's, and Yellow warblers.

Along the river's shallows live crayfish and freshwater shellfish. They provide food for Raccoons. Other mammals, including Coyote, Striped and Spotted skunks, and Badger, drink from the river as well.

Other aspects of the preserve are revealed by walking along the levees. In the North Marsh stand an isolated pair of ancient Valley Oaks splashed white from the droppings of a hundred or more year-round resident Great Blue Herons. In spring these noisy birds fill the sky as they wing back and forth from marsh to nest, bringing food to their hungry chicks. You can hear the heron rookery from a mile away—it sounds like a bunch of quacking Mallards with clothespins on their noses.

By late spring the water in the reservoirs, canals, and marshes has all but disappeared. The cracked, dried bottoms in the canals and reservoirs resemble giant jigsaw puzzles. Raccoons turn over pieces of the solidified mud in search of fish trapped beneath. Any remaining pools of water boil with schools of carp and bluegills gasping their last. Egrets and Great Blue and Black-crowned Night herons find the pickings easy. No wonder Creighton Ranch supports the greatest concentrated population of Black-crowneds in the United States.

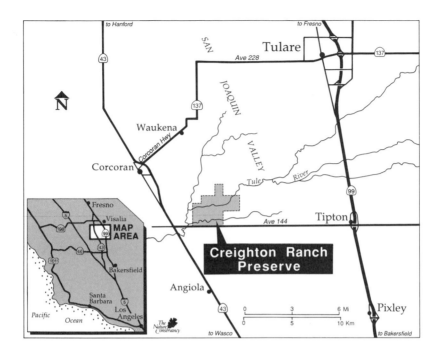

Follow the main levee road through the preserve and you'll walk past the Little and Big reservoirs. They are ringed by thick clumps of tule. Indians relied on the ubiquitous plant for nearly everything, making boats, houses, and mats out of the tall green stalks. They even climbed the clumps for use as hunting perches.

The reservoirs are filled with water from about October to late April. More than a dozen species of duck have been sighted on them: Wood Duck, American Wigeon, Gadwall, Green-winged and Cinnamon teal, Northern Shoveler, Canvasback, and Redhead, to name a few. Other waterfowl that rely on the ponds are Canada Goose, Ring-necked Duck, Common Merganser, and Ruddy Duck. Shorebirds and wading birds are also in attendance in the wet months. Black-necked Stilt nest here as do Pied-billed Grebe, American Bittern, Common Moorhen, and Virginia Rail. Whimbrel, Black-bellied Plover, and Sandhill Crane are some of the more unusual visitors to look for.

Toward the end of the road, you'll reach a stand of Valley Oak. Fewer than eighty of these magnificent trees have survived since the 1920s. Beneath their pendant branches thrives an almost impenetrable understory of Mule Fat, sagebrush, and Stinging Nettle.

Time your walk so you're heading back at dusk, when the animal life is most active. Thousands of Red-winged Blackbirds noisily return from the fields to bed down in the Cattails. Great Horned Owls hoot from perches on the Valley Oaks, while Common Barn Owls swoop after restless blackbirds. Ducks and geese seem to argue and gossip as they settle down for the night. Finally, as dusk turns to evening, American Bitterns begin to pump. Their pulsing call, "choonk-oong-ka-choonk-oong-ka-choonk," fills the air, giving rhythm to the mournful howls of Coyotes baying at the moon.

Creighton Ranch Checklist

INFORMATION

Please call ahead before visits from October 1 to January 31. For more information, and to arrange a visit, contact the preserve manager at P.O. Box 3840, Visalia, CA 93278; (209) 627-4328.

SIZE

3,280 acres

SEASONAL HIGHLIGHTS

Wildflower display and vernal pools in spring; nesting and migrating birds from late April to early May, and in September; waterfowl from October to March.

WEATHER

Desertlike climate; summers are hot and dry, and winters cool and foggy.

ON-SITE FACILITIES

Self-guided nature trail, interpretive center, picnic tables, restrooms.

NEAREST OFF-SITE FACILITIES

5 miles away in Corcoran

EQUIPMENT

good walking shoes
binoculars
water
sun protection in summer

TIME REQUIRED

3 to 4 hours

DIRECTIONS

From Los Angeles, travel north on Highway 99 to Highway 190 at Tipton. Drive west approximately 10 miles on Highway 190 (also called Ave. 144) to the Creighton Ranch Preserve entrance, located on the north side of the road where it crosses Lakeland Canal. From San Francisco, take Interstate 5 south, then Highway 152 east to Highway 99. Travel south to Highway 43 (turnoff in Selma). Then drive south on Highway 43 past Hanford and Corcoran to Ave. 144 (Tipton Highway). Go east 2 miles to the preserve gate.

FOURTEEN

Pixley Vernal Pools

Trial by Fire

THOUGH A relatively small preserve at 40 acres, Pixley Vernal Pools envelops many of the natural features once common to the grasslands of the southern Central Valley. Here native grasses and endemic wildflowers still thrive despite being completely surrounded by mile after cultivated mile of row crops. The protected habitat also serves as a tiny but vital watershed cover and home for a number of native animals.

Located in the southeastern San Joaquin Valley in Tulare County, Pixley Vernal Pools Preserve is a remnant of what this area used to be before mechanized agriculture took over. The loss of native grassland in the past century has been enormous. In the San Joaquin Valley alone, 5.3 million acres have been converted to irrigated farmland, 150,000 acres to dry-farmed grain, and most of the remainder to grazing land. In the Tulare Basin, less than two percent of the original 664,000 acres of native grassland survives.

Pixley Vernal Pools escaped the plow thanks to the foresight and generosity of a local grape grower and botanist, Jack Zaninovich. He discovered the untamed field in the early 1960s and fell in love with its pristine beauty. Zaninovich purchased the property in order to preserve it. In 1964 he transferred ownership to The Nature Conservancy.

As its name implies, the preserve contains a number of vernal pools, shallow depressions in the underlying impervious hardpan. Between 25 and 75 of these so-called "hog wallows" exist—the number depends on the amount of rainfall each year. The valley's climate is typically Mediterranean with hot, dry summers and cool, moist winters. Rainfall is scant, averaging 6.9 inches per year, nearly identical to totals in the Mojave Desert. What keeps Tulare Basin from resembling the desert is the presence of tule fog in winter. This dense ground fog has a moderating climatic influence on local vegetation.

Vernal pools fill with water during the rainy season. The collected water triggers a growth cycle in a number of endemic plants. Seeds germinate in the water and complete their short life cycle as the water within the pools evaporates. Among the remarkable wildflowers that have adapted to this special habitat are the blue-flowered Downingia, white-flowered Popcorn Flower, and yellow-flowered Goldfields. Because they bloom at different times and at different levels, their showy blossoms form concentric bands of color around the vernal pools as the water recedes.

These three species give the pools their chief color during spring, but many other plants also grow in the surrounding grassland, including the white-petaled Bird's-eye Gilia, Purple Owl's Clover, orange Fiddleneck, yellow and white Butter-and-Eggs (also known as Johnny Tuck), bright purple Blue Dicks, and two species of lupine.

Another species stirred to activity by the water is the Spade-foot Toad. During the hot, dry summers, this unusual amphibian lies buried in the mud, where it awaits the right amount of water to fill the pool so it can hatch, mate, and lay more eggs. Sometimes the toads have to wait as long as three years between adequate rains.

Vernal pools are important to a variety of other animals. Invertebrates, such as fairy shrimp, and many insects require water to complete their life cycles. Ducks and shorebirds find the pools convenient resting and feeding spots during migration.

Red-tailed Hawks and Black-shouldered Kites soar above the grasslands in search of California Ground Squirrels, Black-tailed Hares, rabbits, snakes, and lizards. On high ground, stand long-legged Burrowing Owls. They use the abandoned burrows of mammals for nesting and shelter. In fact, most animal life here dwells underground to escape the heat of summer and cold of winter. Ground squirrels play an indispensable role in digging the burrows; skinks, Darkling Beetles, Black Widows, and Side-blotched Lizards share the abandoned ones.

Pixley Vernal Pools has not completely escaped the influence of introduced species. European annual grasses, such as Red Brome, Soft Chess, Foxtail Fescue, and Hare Barley, are stiff competition for the only common native annual grasses, Alkali Barley and Few-flowered Fescue. Domination by alien annuals also suppresses the growth of other native plants. Succession has led to a "climax community"— in other words, one characterized by low species diversity and low percent composition of native species.

The reason for this involves the build-up of mulch — dead plant parts from previous seasons' growth — on the soil surface and its consequent modification of the microenvironment. Under the mulch layer, native

◄ *Pixley Vernal Pools Preserve*

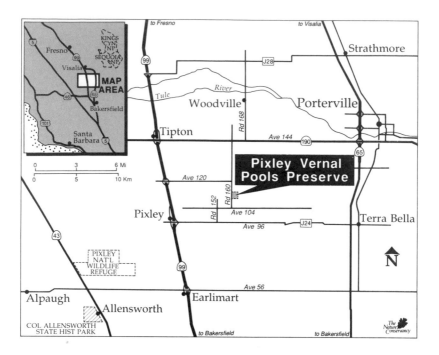

species generally cannot germinate or are unable to grow upward through the mulch to the life-giving sunlight.

In presettlement times, fires and grazing by native animals removed the mulch layer. Range fires swept the valley unsuppressed. Some were started by Yokuts Indians for various reasons; others were caused naturally, frequently by lightning. A fall thunderstorm accompanied by high winds made for fast-moving, quick-burning fires that blazed across the land until quelled by rain or a wet streambed.

Fire increases species diversity in California's grasslands. When the dominant grass is burned, the resulting decline in its composition percentage provides a competitive release for other groups. Realizing that, The Nature Conservancy has been using controlled burning as a management tool to retard alien annuals and help stimulate the growth of many native species.

Prescribed burning at Pixley Vernal Pools has been conducted for the past several years. Burns are scheduled in fall when maximum dryness of the mulch layer coincides with high humidity and cooler temperatures. In other words, the fuel is drier but the burning conditions are safer.

The burns have dramatically increased the cover of native plants in the grassland as well as the number of native species. The vernal pools usually do not burn because of lack of sufficient fuel. However, those that have burned show no apparent adverse effect.

The floral display at Pixley Vernal Pools is brief. Blooming season might last only six weeks. The best time of year to visit is during the months of March, April, and May—it all depends on the rain.

The preserve is readily recognizable. A dirt road rings the fenced property. Take extra care when walking through the property. There are no trails and the pools are particularly sensitive to trampling. By standing on one of the mima mounds, you can look down into the vernal pools and drink in all the colors. The surrounding fields of cultivated green and plowed earth makes the wild and beautiful spectrum even more pronounced.

Pixley Vernal Pools Checklist

INFORMATION

For information, contact the preserve manager at P.O. Box 3840, Visalia, CA 93278; (209) 627-4328.

SIZE

40 acres

SEASONAL HIGHLIGHTS

Early spring for vernal pools and wildflower display.

WEATHER

Hot, dry summers and cool, moist winters. Winter tule fogs are common. Rain averages 8 inches per year.

ON-SITE FACILITIES

None. No shade.

NEAREST OFF-SITE FACILITIES

5 miles west in Pixley

EQUIPMENT

soft-soled shoes
binoculars
magnifying glass

TIME REQUIRED

2 hours

DIRECTIONS

From the north via Highway 99, exit 12 miles south of Tulare on Road 120 and head east. Stay on 120 for five miles and turn right on Road 160. Take 160 south 1.8 miles and watch for the preserve on the left. From the south, take Highway 99 north to County Highway J24. Head east for three miles to its junction with Road 152. Turn left and go one mile north to Road 104. Turn right and drive another mile east until you reach Road 160. Turn left. The preserve is located on the right, 450 yards from the intersection.

California Orcutt Grass

Orcuttia californica

THE VERNAL pools of California are the only places in the world you'll find the native annual grass *Orcuttia* growing in its natural state.

All seven species (*Orcuttia californica, O. viscida, O. pilosa, O. tenuis, O. greenei, O. mucronata*, and *O. fragilis*) of this fascinating genus are considered rare and endangered by the California Native Plant Society. With the exception of the monotypic genus *Neostapfia*, the *Orcuttia* species form a distinct group within the grass family, with no apparent affinities to any other grasses. To botanists, that implies an ancient origin for this unique group.

Unlike other native grasses found in North America, *Orcuttia* are covered by stalked glandular hairs that secrete a droplet of sticky, aromatic, bitter-tasting substance. Apparently this secretion acts as a natural defense mechanism against voracious grasshoppers.

Orcutt grass grows only in the California vernal pools that retain standing water into the late spring or early summer. It is usually found flourishing alone on a bed of barren, cracked mud in the evaporated vernal pool.

Three of the seven species, including *Orcuttia californica*, have an aquatic seedling stage. For them, germination takes place sometime during fall or winter after standing water has been present in the vernal pool for two to four weeks.

After germination, the seedling produces several short leaves and develops a large root system. By midspring, when the water level has decreased, *Orcuttia* produces long, floating leaves that allow the plant to reach direct sunlight for the first time. When the water evaporates completely in late spring or early summer, the plant produces a third type of leaf. At this time, it takes on the appearance of a more typical terrestrial grass.

California Orcutt Grass

Just days after the water evaporates, the first inflorescence appears. Because the plant used its aquatic growth phase to develop its root system and a considerable portion of stem tissue, it can now direct the remainder of its energy toward flowering and seed production, even though soil moisture is in short supply.

The other four species of *Orcuttia* germinate as the last standing water evaporates. They do not possess floating leaves. Once the water is gone, however, the rest of their life history mirrors that of the three aquatic types.

When the water held in the mud of the vernal pool is completely consumed, the grass dies. The plant remains intact, as a dried "skeleton" attached to the bed of the pool. When the first heavy rainstorms of fall arrive, the plant finally disintegrates, dispersing its summer-produced seeds to start the cycle all over again.

FIFTEEN

Paine Wildflower

Under Lonesome Skies

PAINE WILDFLOWER Preserve is an enigmatic place. At first glance, you might wonder why the effort was made to protect this desolate-looking patch of low-lying scrubland located in the southern San Joaquin Valley. Biologically, it doesn't appear to offer much: outward signs of wildlife are few, the flora hardly seems diverse, and aesthetically . . . well, it certainly lacks the visceral punch of a granite-capped Sierra peak or the easy beauty of a sun-kissed shoreline. But on closer inspection, the magic of Paine Preserve reveals itself. Slowly, subtly. Layer by life-sustaining layer. The more you look, the more you'll see.

Until the most extensive system of aqueducts on earth and wholesale agriculture turned the rest of the Central Valley into the world's salad bowl, Paine Preserve was not unique. Now it is. A 600-acre remnant of the way a significant portion of the valley used to be, Paine is an excellent example of the alkali playa habitat.

The landscape consists of gently sloping mounds of wind-deposited, very light and sandy loam, of low hummocks, and a series of slight depressions. Total relief is no more than ten feet. The climate is Mediterranean with hot, dry summers and cool, damp winters. Rainfall is scant, averaging only five inches per year—not even enough to support the wide variety of grasses that grow in other sections of the valley. When it does rain, the low areas on the preserve fill with water, forming shallow vernal pools that quickly evaporate, leaving behind expanses of cracked mud.

Sharp contrasts in the soil occur within a very few feet. In the depressions, soils are heavily alkaline. These are surrounded by subalkaline

Paine Wildflower Preserve ▶

Blunt-nosed Leopard Lizard

playa fans and slopes. The soil on the hummocks and low ridges is neutral, and supports a large variety of plants.

The vegetation is a mosaic of Lowland Valley Saltbush Scrub and Northern Hardpan Vernal Pool natural communities. Spiny Saltbush, which grows predominantly on the flat, poorly drained soils, and Common Saltbush, which prefers the drainage of sloping uplands, form the dominant shrubby cover. Soil lichens dot the ground in otherwise bare areas. Perhaps the most distinctive plant is the Alkali Larkspur, a rare endemic of the upper San Joaquin alkali sink. Pale lavender with tall stalks, it is plentiful here, growing in dense colonies beneath the saltbush.

Other alkali-tolerant plants present are Shiny Peppergrass, Pineapple Weed, Alkali Barley, and three or possibly four species of Goldfields. In the neutral soils grow Bird's-eye Gilia, Small Fescue, Chia, phacelia, and Johnny Tuck, among others. Perennials include rare individuals of Pine Bluegrass and abundant clumps of Alkali Sacaton, an impressive bunchgrass that was once a distinctive feature of the broad alkali plains of central Kern County before the advent of wide-scale farming.

The flora supports an amazing number of animal species, including several classified as rare or endangered. The state-listed San Joaquin Antelope Squirrel lives here, along with Deer Mouse, San Joaquin Pocket Mouse, Black-tailed Hare, and Heermann's and San Joaquin kan-

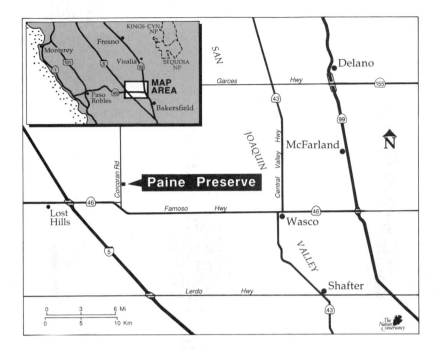

garoo rats. The burrow-dwelling animals form the diet for such birds of prey as Prairie Falcon, Golden Eagle, Burrowing Owl, Northern Harrier, Red-tailed Hawk, and Rough-legged Hawk, as well as for Coyote, Badger, and the federally endangered San Joaquin Kit Fox.

During the wet season, amphibians and aquatic invertebrates breed in temporary standing water, attracting waterfowl, shorebirds, and wading birds. Western Kingbirds, with their gray and yellow feathers, sit on the fences surrounding the preserve, while Western Meadowlarks whistle in the scrub. Flocks of Red-winged, Tri-colored, and Yellow-headed blackbirds travel back and forth between farm and fields.

As the heat of summer approaches, the endangered Blunt-nosed Leopard Lizard stirs, hunting for insects on the sparsely vegetated flatlands. Other reptiles include the Side-blotched Lizard and the Western Whiptail.

The preserve began as a single, 40-acre parcel. Jack Zaninovich and the late Ernest Twisselmann, two long-time valley ranchers who shared a love for the area's unique botany, had to search for more than a year before they could find a representative piece of untilled alkali playa. The Nature Conservancy purchased the land in 1968 with monies donated by Olivia Paine in memory of her husband, Paul. Since then, the Conservancy has added two 160-acre parcels and a 200-acre parcel. Though none of the four adjoin each other now, the hope is to eventually acquire the properties between to create a single 2,000-acre preserve. Working with the sprawling Kern National Wildlife Refuge, located just five and one-half miles north, the preserve would help protect a staircase of habitats—from Lowland Saltbush to Freshwater Marsh.

Late winter through early spring is the perfect time of year to pay a visit to the preserve. Wildflowers are in bloom and Goldfields carpet the prairie floor. As long as there is water in the vernal pools, ducks, geese, and shorebirds are numerous. Songbird migration is at its peak in late April and early May.

Dirt roads surround the parcels. Your arrival will prompt dozens of California Ground Squirrels to scurry across the road as they dash for the cover of the preserve. Their mad scramble is tangible evidence of how plowing leaves no room to hide for burrow-dwelling creatures.

In March, heavy cumulus clouds scud across the sky. You can track their speed by following their shadows across the lonesome prairie. When the wind blows, the hummocks look like ocean chop. Small twisters twirl tumbleweeds and loose earth over the barren spots. Prairie Falcons perform impossible turns and dives as they chase down prey.

Surrounded by cultivated fields, Paine Preserve has a quiet desolation to it, but it positively resounds with echoes of the past. It stands as a time capsule of the original southern San Joaquin Valley landscape.

Paine Wildflower Checklist

INFORMATION

For information contact the pre-serve manager at P.O. Box 3840, Visalia, CA 93278; (209) 627-4328.

SIZE

600 acres

SEASONAL HIGHLIGHTS

Winter raptors; spring wild-flowers and vernal pools.

WEATHER

Mediterranean, with hot, dry summers and cool, damp winters.

ON–SITE FACILITIES

None

NEAREST OFF–SITE FACILITIES

In nearby communities of Wasco and Delano

EQUIPMENT

soft-soled walking shoes
binoculars
magnifying glass
water
sun protection in summer

TIME REQUIRED

2 hours

DIRECTIONS

Take Interstate 5 to Highway 46 near Lost Hills. Head east on 46 for 4.3 miles to its junction with Corcoran Road and turn left. After traveling 2.2 miles, you will come to a poor-quality dirt road that leads off to the right. This road junction is at the southwest corner of the original 40-acre preserve.

SOUTH

SIXTEEN

Kern River

Riparian Repaired

RIPARIAN FORESTS — the lush green woodlands that grow in river floodplains — are among the richest of all habitats. Sadly, they are becoming among the rarest as well, a loss to the encroachment of agriculture, industry, housing, highways, airports, reservoirs and other preemptive uses of once virgin land.

Invasion and alteration of America's forested floodplains have progressed ever since modern man arrived on the scene. To the pioneers, river bottomland was preeminently accessible and easy to cultivate and build upon. Forest was cut for timber and fuel and to make room for farms and towns. Rivers were dammed to provide drinking water and irrigation, and channelized with concrete and rock riprap to prevent flooding and erosion.

Nowhere is the loss of riparian habitat more evident than in California's Great Central Valley. In the 1800s, more than 800,000 acres of forest lined the rivers that drained the Sierra Nevada. Today, only two percent of these woodlands survive, a total of about 12,000 acres. As the riparian habitat has dwindled, so have wildlife populations.

Twenty percent of the state's riverine forest that remains grows along fourteen miles of the South Fork of the Kern River as it spills out of Domeland Wilderness at the southern terminus of the Sierra Nevada and flows into man-made Lake Isabella to the west. One four-mile stretch in particular provides a heartening example of what riches such wild places hold. Here, on 1,127 acres preserved by The Nature Conservancy, dense stands of Fremont Cottonwood and Red Willow still shade the river, providing habitat for an incredible number of animals and over two hundred bird species, including the Yellow-billed Cuckoo, which the state has listed as threatened. Additionally, work is now underway to repair the loss of river woodland by creating even more.

The Kern River Preserve lies within the South Fork, Kern River Valley near the small town of Weldon. The valley is lush and bucolic, blessed with few people, a temperate climate, and a moderate elevation that ranges from 2,600 to 2,700 feet. The river passes through the preserve from east to west. Several small irrigation ditches and beaver ponds are scattered about the land. Fertile alluvial soils, a high water table, and ample sunshine foster a healthy forest mixed with thickets of Mule Fat, Sandbar Willow, Stinging Nettle, and Common Rabbit Brush.

For centuries, Indians of the Tubatalabal tribe roamed this valley, living off its abundant game and plants. They left grinding holes in the granite boulders at the northwestern edge of the preserve. White settlers arrived shortly after 1850. They cleared the land to make pastures and raised cattle and hay. One of these early farmers, Andrew Brown, originally owned the land that now makes up the preserve. A flour mill he built on the property in 1870 still stands today. The local chapter of the Historical Society is currently restoring it.

Agriculture continues to play a major role in the valley. The Conservancy leases out 200 acres of the preserve for cattle grazing and farming. It is also doing some farming of its own, but not the kind you might expect. Instead of sowing oats and alfalfa, Conservancy staff and volunteers have planted rows and rows of cottonwood and willow in an ambitious program designed to expand the existing riparian forest by as many as 300 acres.

The unique reforestation experiment, headed by Dr. Bertin Anderson, got underway in 1986. A test patch of 25 acres was planted with 20-inch cuttings. Drip irrigation from a custom-built system helped get the new plantings established. The trees took root quickly, and growth was explosive. After nearly twelve weeks, the trees were almost six feet tall. The pilot test proved so successful that two more fields totalling 65 acres were planted the following spring. Again, the growth rate averaged over one-half inch a day. The hope is that in a decade the meadows will be filled with 100-foot-tall trees.

The main objective of the program is to enhance Yellow-billed Cuckoo habitat, so the area can support up to twenty pairs of breeding cuckoos. Only nine pairs currently breed here—less than half the number needed to sustain a healthy population. Each pair requires a minimum of 40 acres for foraging. Although there are 800 acres of willows and cottonwoods on the preserve, the forest is confined to a thin, narrow strip. The birds will not travel the length of the corridor to sustain themselves. Widening the riparian gallery could make a difference.

Yellow-billed Cuckoos aren't the only creatures that will benefit from increased riparian habitat. The preserve is also home to several other uncommon species of birds, including the largest population of Willow

Kern River Preserve ▶

Flycatchers in the state. About forty pairs visit the preserve from late April through summer. Yellow-headed and Tri-colored blackbirds, Black-headed and Evening grosbeaks, Lawrence's Goldfinch, White-throated Swift, and four types of wren and four kinds of swallow also rely on the river forest for survival. Wood Ducks nest in the river's backwaters, Brown Towhee feed on wild currants along the banks, and Black-crowned Night Heron, Blue-winged Teal, Mallard, Pintail, and a host of other birds congregate in the ponds.

Because three biogeographical provinces overlap here, the preserve hosts an unusual mix of wildlife. Not only is it influenced by the Central Valley, but also by the Sierra Nevada and the Mojave Desert. On the hillsides overlooking the river grow such desert plants as Beavertail Cactus, while Salt Grass and native Wild Rye Grass—two plants closely associated with the valley—grow in the meadows below. One of the more noteworthy species of plants found at the preserve is the Alkali Mariposa Lily, which grows in the moist meadows alongside the river at the east end of the preserve. You can spot its blossoms in May.

Butterflies are also abundant in great numbers. A hundred species have been identified within a few miles of Lake Isabella. Each year the local chapter of the Xerces Society holds a butterfly count. Several unique species have turned up. The Eunus Skipper was believed to be extinct until 81 were found on the preserve. Another rare find was the San Emigdio Blue.

Mammals of all sizes frequent the preserve: deer, Coyote, Beaver, Long-tailed Weasel, Dusky-footed Wood Rat, and occasionally Black Bear and Mountain Lion. Reptiles include the Gilbert's Skink, Desert Spiny Lizard, and Western Pond Turtle, the only turtle native to interior California. The turtles hibernate in the mud at the bottom of the ponds from November to February.

May is a good time to visit the preserve. Songbirds are in the peak of migration, wildflowers are in full bloom, and the river is bustling with energy. Begin at the Visitor Center. The building once served as the Mountain Hotel in old Kernville, a nearby town that now sits at the bottom of Lake Isabella. A self-guided nature trail begins outside its front door. First stop is a reforested meadow. A forest filled with uniform rows of trees may strike you as unnatural looking, but in a few years the trees will mature and the orchard appearance will disappear.

A stile takes you over a fence erected to protect the young trees from trespassing livestock. Here you enter the original forest. The willows are among the oldest on the property, and in May, the cottonwoods loose a snowstorm of white down. A series of conveniently placed boardwalks carries you over the wetter areas. The plants growing here are predominantly Cattail, tule, and Wild Celery. Azolla, a free-floating water fern, covers the deeper spots. Listen for birdsong—the avian harmony

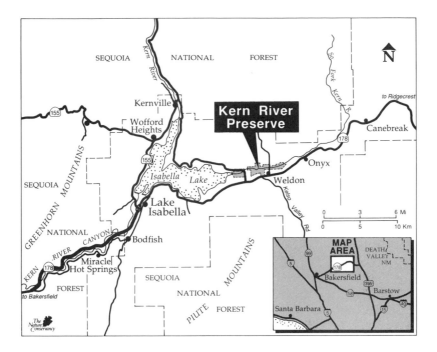

includes House Wren, Song Sparrow, Plain Titmouse, and ten kinds of warblers.

Before looping back to preserve headquarters, the trail leads to river's edge. Tree Swallows—their iridescent bodies gleaming—dart over the river to and from nests they've made in abandoned woodpecker holes. Western Wood Peewees, hidden from view, call shrilly to the babble of the river.

To get a bird's-eye view of the preserve, head down Sierra Way near the property's western boundary and follow the path that begins on the righthand side of the road just after you cross the bridge. The path parallels the river, passing through a jumble of granite—look for the Indian grinding holes—and across a patch of Wild Cucumber or Man Root, a plant named for its large tap root. The river is quiet here, stilled by logs felled by Beaver. The toothy mammals aren't native to the area, but were introduced years ago to the high country by the state. Floods carried them downstream and they became established at lower elevations.

Follow the trail as it gradually climbs the hill. Once you're above tree level, pull up a rock and share the view with the hawks and falcons that roost in nearby crevices. They rely on the vantage point to keep an eye out for prey. You can use it to trace the length of California's longest intact river forest as it winds out of the mountains, stretches across the valley, and disappears into the lapping waters of the reservoir downstream. The thick, green gallery of trees offers a bright picture of hope for hundreds of species of wildlife and future generations to come.

Kern River Checklist

INFORMATION

For information and to arrange a visit, contact the preserve manager at P.O. Box 1662, Weldon, CA 93283; (619) 378-2531.

SIZE

1,127 acres

SEASONAL HIGHLIGHTS

Wildflowers and bird migration in spring; Alkali Mariposa Lily blooms in May; and the annual butterfly count in June.

WEATHER

Desert climate. Arid and hot in summers, cool in winters.

ON-SITE FACILITIES

Visitor Center and self-guided nature trail

NEAREST OFF-SITE FACILITIES

One mile east in Weldon

EQUIPMENT

good walking shoes
binoculars
food and water
mosquito repellant

TIME REQUIRED

Half to full day

DIRECTIONS

From Bakersfield, go east 57 miles on Highway 178 through Kern River Canyon and Lake Isabella areas. Exactly 1.1 miles past the Kernville Airport turnoff, turn left into the preserve. From Mojave Desert, turn west from Highway 14 onto Highway 178. Go over Walker Pass and through communities of Canebreak and Onyx, 30 miles to Weldon. Go one mile past Weldon to preserve entrance on right.

Yellow-billed Cuckoo

Coccyzus americanus

*T*HE TANGLED wooded banks along the South Fork of the Kern River shelter sixteen, possibly seventeen of the most elusive birds in the world, the Yellow-billed Cuckoo. As few as a hundred and no more than three hundred are thought to exist in the entire state.

Western Yellow-billed Cuckoos haven't always been so rare. As recently as sixty years ago, they were a common sight west of the Rockies. In 1865 ornithologist James G. Cooper found cuckoos in trees along Sacramento streets. At the turn of the century, naturalist Antoine Jay recorded more than forty nests in what is now downtown Los Angeles. Although no complete census was taken in that era, experts believe California then had at least 70,000 breeding pairs.

The Yellow-billed Cuckoo, named for its yellow mandible, is a member of a family numbering 128 species worldwide. In North America, there are four other types of cuckoo, including the Greater Roadrunner.

The western variety resembles the more common eastern subspecies but is paler and larger, with a heavier bill. It is comparable in size to the Scrub Jay and has a greenish back, rusty-red wings, and large black and white spots on the underside of its long tail.

Unlike European cuckoos, which lay their eggs in other birds' nests and leave rearing to unsuspecting foster parents, the Yellow-billed builds its own nest and raises its own young. The time from egg-laying to fledging is shorter for this cuckoo than any other bird species.

The cuckoo synchronizes its nesting at a particular site with the hatching of that area's most common insect. Favorite foods are caterpillars, katydids, and tree frogs. The bird can increase its clutch size in times of abundant food supply, and hatches its eggs in stages to vary the size and age of its brood. And to protect older nestlings when food sources run short, the cuckoo sometimes expels its youngest from the nest. These behaviors

Yellow-billed Cuckoo

suggest that the cuckoo is adapted to take advantage of short-term, abundant food supply and may be very sensitive to food scarcity.

Yellow-billeds summer in North America and winter in South America. They dwell exclusively in the forests of river floodplains — and that's why they have declined at such a rapid rate.

The bird's summer home is fast becoming among the rarest habitat in North America, a casualty of a civilization that relentlessly commandeers more and more space for agricultural, industrial, and urban development. Nationally, some 700,000 acres of wetlands are being converted each year. Only two percent remains of the cuckoo's native habitat in California.

The Kern River Preserve represents twenty percent of the bird's available habitat. To increase this habitat and thus help protect the Yellow-billed, the California Nature Conservancy staff and volunteers have undertaken a novel restoration project aimed at expanding riparian forest along the Kern River. Work is in progress to plant 300 acres with cottonwoods and willows, which, it is hoped, will double the resident cuckoo population by the year 2000.

SEVENTEEN

Carrizo Plain

California's Serengeti

I N THE *spring, native bunch grasses, reaching as tall as the side of a horse, grew thick on the undulating land turning to naturally cured hay in the summer. Wild horses, elk, deer and antelope were abundant in the plain and large flocks of sandhill cranes spent each winter at Soda Lake . . .*

—San Luis Obispo Tribune, 1886

A century after that report was filed, Carrizo Plain remains remarkably the same. True, it has not escaped untouched. Livestock and dry farming have had some impact on native grasses, and the Tule Elk and Pronghorn both needed to be reintroduced. But in winter, the sky still fills with thousands of Lesser and Greater Sandhill cranes, and San Joaquin Kit Foxes still give birth in the spring.

Carrizo Plain represents the largest remaining example of San Joaquin Valley habitat. Of all of California's biogeographic provinces, only the valley is left unrepresented by a major park or preserve. At 180,000 acres, the plain is our last chance at protecting one of California's richest ecosystems. Not coincidentally, it is the venue for the single, largest habitat preservation project in the state ever attempted. By 1997, The Nature Conservancy, working in concert with state and federal agencies, private landowners, ranchers, and the oil and gas industry, hopes to protect Carrizo in a project so large it has been called a macropreserve. The process is currently underway, and already over 80,000 acres have been acquired and preserved.

Carrizo Plain is one of those rare places in California that time and progress seem to have overlooked. Located in eastern San Luis Obispo County, the 8-mile-wide by 50-mile-long expanse of arid scrub and grassland is hemmed in by two ranges, the Caliente to the south and west and the Temblor to the north and east.

The infamous San Andreas Fault—at 650 miles, it is the longest contiguous earthquake fault in the state—borders the plain on the east and is responsible for the area's creation. Carrizo was formed some thirty million years ago when movements along the San Andreas and San Juan faults caused the area in between to subside, forming a basin. Simultaneously, the ancestral Temblor and Caliente mountains were rapidly pushing upward. This combination of basin subsidence and mountain uplift accelerated erosion. For ages, sediments washed from the mountains, filling the basin now known as the Carrizo Plain.

The entire plain was once a vast prehistoric lake, filled by runoff waters from the adjacent slopes. As sediments built up over geologic time, the lake became shallower, increased in salinity, and became more prone to drying in the summer. Today, though drastically reduced in size, Soda Lake, at 3,000 acres, is the largest remaining natural Alkali Wetland in central and southern California. So rare is it, in fact, that the U.S. Fish and Wildlife Service has ranked it among the most important of the state's 49 rarest wildlife habitats.

Other distinct habitats in Carrizo Plain—Alkali Sink, Saltbush Scrub, and Annual Grassland—together form a unique ecosystem, one of the most complex in the world. The plain supports the most diverse and largest concentration of rare and endangered vertebrate species in all of California: San Joaquin Kit Fox, Blunt-nosed Leopard Lizard, Giant Kangaroo Rat, San Joaquin Antelope Squirrel, Greater Sandhill Crane, American Peregrine Falcon, and Bald Eagle. In recent times the California Condor foraged for food here. In addition, three plants are candidates for the federal endangered species list: Forked Fiddleneck, Lost Hills Saltbush, and Congdon's Eatonella.

Besides the threatened or endangered species, Carrizo Plain provides habitat on a seasonal or year-round basis for at least 11 species of reptiles, 100 species of birds, and 40 species of mammals.

The plain is critical wintering habitat for 4,000 to 6,000 rare Sandhill Cranes, one-fourth of the total California wintering population. These large, spectacular flyers congregate around Soda Lake and forage in neighboring fields and grasslands. The lake is vital to their survival, because wintering habitat to the east in the Central Valley proper has been dramatically reduced for agriculture. Moreover, Carrizo has been called by some biologists the largest raptor wintering and feeding area in the whole state. Golden Eagles, Swainson's Hawks, Prairie Falcons, Merlins, Short-eared and Burrowing owls, and Northern Harriers are among the notable birds of prey that frequent the site.

Carrizo is special not only for the numbers of unique species it supports, but for being one of the few places in California where normal

◄ *Carrizo Plain Preserve*

ecological relationships still exist between several endemic species. Here San Joaquin Kit Fox, Blunt-nosed Leopard Lizard, and Giant Kangaroo Rat persist in healthy numbers. The kit fox and leopard lizard depend on the kangaroo rat—the foxes eat them and the lizards use their burrows for cover. This natural ecological web has been torn in other areas of the Central Valley. Densities of all three strictly San Joaquin Valley species are not high enough to sustain their interdependent relationship; common widespread vertebrates have moved in and replaced them.

Animal densities continue at relatively high levels on the Carrizo Plain, due in part to the region's isolation. Over the years the Temblor Range has acted as something of a barrier, making access and importation of water for agriculture difficult. As a result, settlement remained exceptionally low at Carrizo at the same time it boomed in the Central Valley just to the east. Agriculture generally has been limited to a handful of ranches mainly occupied with raising cattle and sheep. Cultivated fields are largely concentrated on the west side of the basin. Wheat and barley are the main crops.

In the centuries that preceded European settlement, Carrizo Plain was an important place for the Chumash Indians. Numerous occupation sites have been identified, one containing over fifty very large bedrock mortars. The plain is also rich in Indian rock art with an astonishing range of complexity. At a large outcropping of boulders that forms a natural amphitheatre, forty-five separate painted panels have been recorded. These pictographs have suffered greatly at the hands of vandals; much has been lost. Many main characters who play a role in Chumash myth and religion are represented: Coyote and Lizard, as well as bears, snakes, and other creatures.

Carrizo Plain has long been a spiritual site for California Indians— spoken of as a place where "Great Spirits" dwelled. Legend held that if someone ventured into the valley, the earth would tremble violently because the spirits were angry. When Spanish missionaries learned of the belief, they called the place Los Temblores, meaning "the tremblings." No doubt seismic activity occurring along the San Andreas Fault had something to do with the legend's origin.

Late winter to early spring is a good time to visit the plain: Soda Lake is usually filled with water, the cranes are present, and the daytime temperatures are agreeable. Cold nights prevail; Carrizo is the only California location west of the Sierra to record subzero temperatures regularly. Summers tend to be hot and dry, and temperatures often exceed 100 degrees. The self-guided nature trail along the western edge of Soda Lake provides a perfect overview of all four of Carrizo's habitats. Variety in elevation of the terrain above lake level produces profound difference in soil moisture and alkalinity. Within the space of several paces, you can follow the trail through the different plant communities, each higher and dryer than the next.

The first you'll encounter is Alkali Wetland. Soda Lake and the surrounding smaller ponds generally flood with the onset of winter rains and retain water from December to April or May. The ponds become thick with such aquatic plants as Horned Pondweed, a valuable food for waterfowl. American Wigeon, Canvasback Duck, Eared and Pied-billed grebes, Green-winged Teal, Pintail, Tundra Swan, White-fronted Goose, and Wilson's Phalarope are some of the birds that frequent the lake.

American Avocet, Black-necked Stilt, Greater Yellowlegs, Long-billed Curlew, Snowy Plover, and Whimbrel feed along the shoreline. Sandhill Cranes usually arrive in late October, and their population peaks in January. Sandhills are extremely sensitive to human disturbance and require at least 500 yards of flat, open space for roosting areas. The shallow, isolated waters of Soda Lake provide the ideal habitat.

Immediately adjacent to the wetland is the Alkali Sink. This habitat once occurred widely in the Central Valley, but is now extremely rare in California. Salt-tolerant plants, such as Salt Grass, Iodine Bush, Alkali Heath, and the rare and endangered Lost Hills Saltbush, grow in a narrow band. Because the sink habitat is a transition zone between the aquatic and upland vegetation types, it is visited by many animal species. Watch for Bald Eagle, Northern Harrier, and Short-eared Owl, only a few of the species that routinely hunt the alkali flats.

Saltbush Scrub comes next. The flat, salty ground is covered predominantly with Spiny Saltbush and is scattered with patches of Western Larkspur, Goldfields, and Common Saltbush.

Elevations only very slightly higher give way to Annual Grassland. Originally, these vast expanses were covered with native bluegrass, a perennial bunchgrass, but introduced species such as Red Brome and Red-stem Filaree now dominate. In areas protected from heavy grazers, you might find several interesting shrubs and rare plants, including Anderson Desert Thorn, Mormon Tea, Alkali Goldenbush, Common Fiddleneck, and the rare Cottony Buckwheat.

The grassland is prime habitat for most of Carrizo's rare and endangered animals. San Joaquin Kit Foxes are largely nocturnal, but the pups often play around the entrance to their den in broad daylight. San Joaquin Antelope Squirrels dig their burrows under shrubs. They come out in the day. Blunt-nosed Leopard Lizards hibernate during the winter months, and during breeding season—late spring—males defend areas against other males by displaying a brilliant pink color to warn intruders. If this fails, a chase ensues.

At the north end of the plain, in California Valley, two former resident species, which were hunted out at the turn of the century, have returned. In February 1987, the state Department of Fish and Game relocated thirty-nine Pronghorn; two herds of Tule Elk were reintroduced during the preceding two years. If plans to establish the plain as a macropreserve

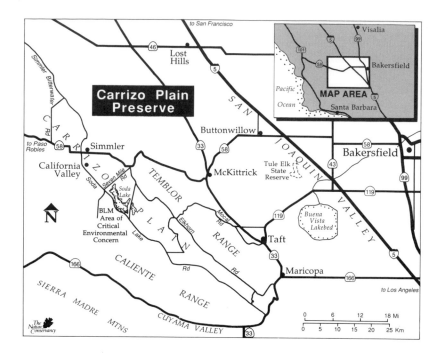

succeed, it should only be a matter of time before these animals thunder in great herds across this California Serengeti, as they did a century ago.

Carrizo Plain Checklist

INFORMATION

For information contact the pre-serve manager at 849 Monterey Street #210, San Luis Obispo, CA 93401; (805) 546-8378.

SIZE

180,000 acres (proposed)

SEASONAL HIGHLIGHTS

Sandhill Cranes late October through February; wildflowers and birds in spring; raptors and waterfowl in winter.

WEATHER

Arid with 8 inches of rainfall per year. Cold nights, cool days, and moist in winter; hot and dry in summer when temperatures can exceed 100 degrees.

ON-SITE FACILITIES

Self-guided nature trail at Soda Lake

NEAREST OFF-SITE FACILITIES

In Santa Margarita to the west, McKittrick to the east.

EQUIPMENT

good walking shoes
binoculars
food and water
sun protection
seasonably appropriate clothing

TIME REQUIRED

Half day

DIRECTIONS

Via Highway 101, take Highway 58 east. Head east through Santa Margarita to California Valley. Turn right on County Road (Soda Lake Road) and head south to Soda Lake. Via Highway 99, take Highway 119 west. At Taft, head south on Highway 33 through Maricopa to either Elkhorn Grade Road (1.6 miles from Maricopa) or continue farther southwest to Soda Lake Road at Reyes Station. Head north to Soda Lake.

SPECIAL SPECIES

San Joaquin Kit Fox
Vulpes macrotis mutica

A MEMBER OF the dog family, the kit fox is one of the smallest species of fox in the world. No bigger than a housecat, an adult weighs on the average five pounds and measures twenty inches. That's about twenty-five percent smaller than the more common Gray Fox.

Despite its diminutive appearance, the kit fox is a striking animal. The foot-long tail is tipped in black, its pelage is the color of California's golden hills, and belly fur is cloud white. Most conspicuous are its ears. At nearly three and one-half inches long, they are relatively enormous, dwarfing the rest of a fist-sized skull. Some biologists suggest they are nature's way of helping the fox dissipate heat.

Eight subspecies of kit fox have been identified in North America; three of them live in Mexico. The most common U.S. subspecies is the Desert Kit Fox. Another subspecies, the Long-eared Kit Fox of Southern California, was driven to extinction shortly after the turn of the century. The San Joaquin subspecies is similar in appearance to other kit foxes, but larger in size.

Kit foxes breed in December and January and are often said to be monogamous and to mate for life. Field observers, however, have noted plenty of incidences of polygamy. It is believed gestation lasts from 49 to 56 days, but no one really knows for sure. Four to five puppies usually make a litter, but no more than five percent live long enough to reach sexual maturity at 22 months. According to researchers, that's typical for a carnivore of this kind.

Vixens rarely leave the den while suckling the pups. Males do most of the hunting during this period. Later, both parents provide food until the pups start to forage at three to four months of age. Pups emerge from the den at about one month and spend several hours each day playing outside the entrance. By October the family groups generally split up;

San Joaquin Kit Fox

pups disperse beyond their parents' home range. Though kit foxes have lived ten to twelve years in zoos, a lifespan of seven years is thought to be average in the wild.

Habitat for the San Joaquin Kit Fox is Saltbush Scrub and grassland. Rabbits and kangaroo rats provide the nighttime hunter with food. Because its supply of prey is dependent on a plentiful source of native vegetation, the fox is acutely sensitive to habitat conversion, especially the kind associated with agriculture.

Originally, the San Joaquin Kit Fox was a widely distributed predator in the semi-arid Central Valley. Starting in the early 1900s, however, the region was transformed into a modern-day Valley of the Nile through the construction of an elaborate series of aqueducts. Industry and urbanism accompanied agricultural development, hastening an increasing rate of habitat loss that eventually led to a drastic decline in kit fox population.

The fox's former range—a territory that once stretched 400 miles and encompassed 14 separate counties—has been greatly reduced. From

1960 to 1970, there was a 34 percent loss of habitat alone. Today less than seven percent of all arable lands in the southern part of the Central Valley remain untilled. According to the U.S. Fish and Wildlife Service, the kit fox has suffered a 20 to 43 percent decline in the past half century. Wildlife biologists believe fewer than 7,000 survive in the state today.

The San Joaquin Kit Fox was listed as endangered in 1966 under the federal Endangered Species Act. Five years later it was classified as rare under California law.

EIGHTEEN

Desert Tortoise

Gaining Ground

THE MOJAVE Desert's power is stark, quiet, palpable. A land of extremes, it is sizzling in summer, freezing in winter. There is little shade from the sun, no shelter from the wind.

One of the most forbidding places on earth, the Mojave can also be incredibly enchanting, especially in March, April, and May. Winter rains set wildflowers blazing across the scrub-studded flats and rolling hills. The fringes of leaves on Joshua Trees rustle like a hula dancer's grass skirt. Migrant songbirds color the gray-green Creosote Bush landscape with feathery splashes of red, blue, and yellow.

Spring is also the time when the Mojave's most enduring resident emerges from its burrow after an eight-month wait to feed on flowering gilias, phacelias, Desert-dandelions, Blazing Stars, and Desert Star Flowers. The burly Desert Tortoise lumbers across the relentless land as it has for the past two million years.

Before man arrived, this heaviest of Southwest reptiles ranged from the northern reaches of the Mojave to the southern Sonoran Desert. Some places in the western Mojave were once habitat to 2,000 tortoises per square mile. Today such densities no longer exist. High density populations of 200 to 400 tortoises per square mile are confined to a handful of ever-diminishing habitats scattered throughout the west. Populations have declined dramatically in most places, and tortoises have been extirpated from significant parts of their geographic range. A combination of agricultural, industrial, and residential development has usurped the ancestral home of California's official state reptile. Gas pipelines, aqueducts, and highways have fragmentized its habitat even further.

One of the few places the tortoise still holds fast is the Desert Tortoise Natural Area, a 39-square-mile natural area, located near the town of California City just two hours by freeway from downtown Los Angeles. The site supports the highest known density of Desert Tortoises anywhere.

The idea of creating such a preserve was first conceived by Dr. Kristin Berry, the world's foremost authority on the Desert Tortoise. She grew concerned about the reptile's welfare while conducting a study for the California Department of Transportation. In 1971 Dr. Berry proposed to the Bureau of Land Management that it set aside ten square miles of prime habitat for the tortoise. The following year the Bureau responded by posting almost thirty square miles as closed to off-road vehicles.

ORVs crush tortoises. They also collapse their burrows. Without shelter, a tortoise will die in the blistering sun. Sheep grazing is also detrimental, for it causes the loss of critical forage, destruction of burrows, trampling of small tortoises, and damage to perennial shrubs used for cover from predators and weather. The sheep compete with the tortoise for its key foods: annual plants and winter annual forbs.

To help protect the Desert Tortoise and maintain the natural density and diversity of the plant and animal life in the area, a group of concerned people from government agencies, academic institutions, turtle and tortoise clubs, and conservation organizations formed the Desert Tortoise Preserve Committee. Their first goal was to get the BLM-designated area fenced to keep out ORVs and livestock. They succeeded. In 1977, a wire mesh fence, which permits free passage of all wildlife, was installed around most of the preserve's perimeter.

In 1976, the Desert Tortoise Preserve Committee became a special project committee with The Nature Conservancy. Since that time, the Conservancy, the State Wildlife Conservation Board, the BLM, and the Preserve Committee have acquired 6.5 square miles of land within the Desert Tortoise Natural Area. The Conservancy and these groups now focus on acquiring the remaining 9.6 square miles of private inholdings.

The preserve protects much more than the Desert Tortoise. Four distinct plant communities support 27 other species of reptiles, 23 species of mammals, 29 species of breeding birds in addition to many migrants, and over 160 species of flowering plants. The state-listed rare Mojave Ground Squirrel depends on the preserve for survival, as does the Golden Eagle, Desert Kit Fox, and the Burrowing Owl, blue-listed by the Audubon Society.

The preserve is primarily made up of shrub-covered flats and low, rolling hills dissected by dry washes and wash stringers that sometimes carry flash floods during the rainy season. There are also about three square miles of steep, rocky canyons. Elevations range from 1,920 to 3,100 feet.

Temperatures can fluctuate 50 degrees in the summer, reaching a high of 110 degrees. In winter, they range from 15 to 57 degrees. The Mojave freezes about 80 days a year. Average annual precipitation measures

◄ *Desert Tortoise Preserve*

between two and five inches. Generally, rain falls between November and February. Winds can howl in excess of 70 miles per hour.

Of the four plant communities, Creosote Bush Scrub is by far the most common. It covers roughly 30 square miles. In the understory grow 15 species of small perennial shrubs, including Burrobush, Goldenhead, Cheese Brush, Winterfat, Spiny Hopsage, and Anderson Desert Thorn. The latter produces bright red berries. Indian Ricegrass and Desert Needlegrass are two common perennial grasses.

Creosote Bush also forms the upper story in the Creosote Bush Scrub/Rocky Slopes and Canyon plant community. Here, the understory comprises California Buckwheat, Nevada Joint-fir, and Tereteleaved Rubberbrush. Mojave Horsebrush grows in the washes.

Joshua Tree Woodland is limited to the higher elevations on the western edge of the Rand Mountains. In spring the understory is colored by showy three-foot-high Mojave Aster and Desert Candle.

In the washes and lower fans on the preserve's northern boundaries, you'll find Saltbush Scrub. Common Saltbush, Scalebroom, Thurber Sandpaper Bush, Shadscale, and Mojave Saltbush are the most common shrubs.

A visit to the Desert Tortoise Natural Area preserve is best made in spring when temperatures are most agreeable to animal and plant life, as well as to people. You'll be able to see the Desert Tortoise outside its burrow in the morning and late afternoon. From mid-June through February, it is usually deep in its burrow and is seldom seen.

Begin your trip at the interpretive center. The covered kiosk contains illustrated displays explaining the site's natural history. A series of connecting nature trail loops starts here. Pick up brochures for the self-guided trails at the start of the Main Loop Trail. The Discovery Trail (1.75 miles long and requiring an hour or two to complete) has no interpretive material.

The Main Loop Trail takes you through a Creosote Bush Scrub community. Keep an eye out at the base of the Creosote Bushes. Desert Tortoises have dug burrows there, and in spring they may be resting on pallets they've scraped in front of burrow entrances. Abandoned burrows house other reptiles, including Zebra-tailed, Long-nosed Leopard, and Side-blotched lizards, and Red Racer, Common Kingsnake, Gopher, Glossy, and Long-nosed snakes. Be aware! Rattlers live here, too. Look for Sidewinder and Mojave Rattlesnake in the open or under bushes.

Rodents appear to have dug holes everywhere. Large holes are occupied by White-tailed Antelope Squirrel, Mojave Ground Squirrel, and Merriam's Kangaroo Rat, whereas Long-tailed Pocket Mouse, Little Pocket Mouse, and Southern Grasshopper Mouse dwell in the smaller ones.

Some birds you might see in the bush include Le Conte's Thrasher, Ash-throated Flycatcher, Say's Phoebe, Horned Lark, Cactus Wren, and

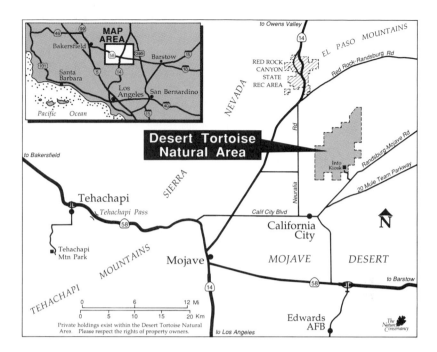

Loggerhead Shrike. Turkey Vulture, Red-tailed Hawk, and Golden
Eagle soar in the open sky while Greater Roadrunner, Gambel's Quail,
and Chukar stick to the ground.

Take your time as you walk. Be patient and you'll see more, experience
more. The pace of life in the desert mimics that of the Desert Tortoise —
slow, purposeful, deliberate. By conserving its resources, the tortoise
has been able to survive for two million years. Surely there's a lesson here
for all of us to learn.

Desert Tortoise Checklist

INFORMATION

For information, contact the Desert Tortoise Preserve Committee, Inc., P.O. Box 453, Ridgecrest, CA 93555.

SIZE

39 square miles

SEASONAL HIGHLIGHTS

Tortoises and wildflowers from mid–March through May

WEATHER

Desert climate: hot and dry in summer when temperatures can exceed 100 degrees, cool in winter.

ON–SITE FACILITIES

Interpretive kiosk, restrooms, shaded benches, self-guided nature trails

NEAREST OFF–SITE FACILITIES

5 miles away in California City

EQUIPMENT

good walking shoes or hiking
  boots
binoculars
plenty of water
hat and sunscreen

TIME REQUIRED

2 to 3 hours

DIRECTIONS

From Los Angeles, travel northwest on Interstate 5 to its intersection with Highway 14. Head east on 14 through the town of Mojave. At California City Blvd., turn right and travel through California City to Randsburg-Mojave Road. Entrance to preserve is 5½ miles from California City.

Desert Tortoise

Xerobates agassizii

A SPECIES OF antiquity, the Desert Tortoise has survived for more than two million years, lumbering across a habitat that ranges from the western reaches of the Mojave to the southern Sonoran Desert. The patient animal is truly a master at adapting to climatic extremes. Active only five to ten percent of the time, the tortoise spends most of life in the shelter of a burrow dug in the desert floor, where it lives on energy stored in its tissues as fat and on water recycled through its bladder.

During spring, when temperatures are mild and food abundant, the tortoise emerges to forage on wildflowers and annual and perennial grasses. It retreats to the cool of its burrow when the summer sun bakes the ground to a blistering 130 degrees. Summer rains bring the tortoise out to drink water in self-dug depressions and to eat dried forbs. Throughout the cold winter season it hibernates as temperatures drop to below 15 degrees.

The Desert Tortoise, which weighs on average seven pounds at maturity, has a high, domed carapace that can grow over a foot long. This shell, along with a leathery skin, keeps it from dehydrating and gives protection from most of its predators, with the exception of man. A Desert Tortoise reaches sexual maturity between 14 and 20 years of age. Clutch size averages three to five eggs, but only an estimated one to five percent of the hatchlings survive to breed.

These tortoises have long been prized as pets. Wildlife biologists estimate that between 1880 and 1970, five to eight million tortoises were taken from the desert by collectors. In fact, more Desert Tortoises may live in people's backyards than in the wild. In the Los Angeles basin alone, for instance, Fish and Game biologists estimate 20,000 tortoises are kept as pets.

In 1961, California made it illegal to take the tortoises (it is the official

Desert Tortoise

state reptile), and Utah and Nevada eventually followed suit. But Arizona permits a bag limit of one tortoise per person, even though a recent population study shows the tortoise there to be in an threatened state. Unfortunately, illegal collecting still takes place in all four states. Those unaware of the law, or just unthinking, are usually at fault—a vacationing family, perhaps, who spots a tortoise alongside a desert road and decides to take it home—but commercial poaching does occur.

Santa Cruz Island

Sanctuary in the Sea

PERHAPS NOTHING is so mystical as an island. In the Spanish novel, California was a strange and wonderful island, if fictitious, teeming with wealth and life never before seen. Recently, some science fiction writers have embraced islands as settings for wild and wondrous tales of giant organisms and long-lost life forms. As it turns out, neither the Spanish novelists of the old world nor modern-day sci-fi hacks have missed the mark. Santa Cruz Island is all these things: home to life forms both giant and minuscule, a setting for unique species, and a miniature California overrun with wonderful sights.

Santa Cruz Island, the largest of the eight Southern California islands, encompasses 62,000 acres. As part of the Transverse Ranges, the island lies parallel to the Santa Barbara coast at a distance of 23 miles. It gives all the appearances of mountaintops thrusting out of the sea, and the island's hikers can verify that feeling. Expanses of flat ground characterize both the island's central valley, an earthquake-fault derived feature that cleaves the island in two, and the marine terraces that ring the island, ancient beaches created when waves lapped high on the island slopes. The remainder of the island is steep, with several peaks exceeding 2,000 feet in elevation and huge seacliffs guarding many of the marine terraces.

The island's geological history remains cloudy. Underwater volcanoes, active from 20 to 12 million years ago, oozed pile after pile of cake-batter lava, forming basalt deposits over 7,000 feet thick. In other areas of the seafloor, sediments accumulated in deep basins and consolidated under immense pressure into soft rock. Still other masses of rock emerged along fault lines from deep within the earth to surface on the island's south flank. This unlikely collection of igneous, sedimentary, and metamorphic rock eventually emerged from the sea to present geologists with one of the great head-scratching problems in Southern California.

The great variety of rock types generates several different landforms and soils, which in turn support spectacular biological diversity. Santa

Santa Cruz Island Preserve

Cruz Island hosts over 625 types of plants, 217 species of birds, and 19 species of native reptiles, amphibians, and terrestrial mammals.

Visitors to the island, glancing back at the distant mainland shores and forward at the wealth of species on the island slopes, inevitably wonder, "How did all these plants and animals get here?" In the study of island biogeography, this is the million-dollar question. Possible answers are as numerous as the myriad species. For the plants, only three transportation possibilities exist: wind, water, and animals.

The prevailing wind whips across the ocean from the northwest, slingshots around Point Conception, and rushes against the island with

Santa Cruz Ironweed

enthusiasm on most days of the year. During autumn, though, this rou-
tine is often interrupted by a very different set of conditions: warm,
clear, brick-dry air from the Southwest deserts hurries to the coast,
squeezing through mountain passes and fanning out across the Santa
Barbara Channel in great rattling gusts. These famous Santa Ana winds
play havoc with mainland civilization, toppling utility poles and over-
turning trucks in the extreme. They also blow vast quantities of living
things out to sea. Seeds and other plant fragments can sail for miles on
hurricane-force winds, and many birds are also carried away. Most of
this biological rain falls into the sea to perish. But the broad face of Santa
Cruz Island catches many of these airborne travelers, some of which
perish nevertheless, but some of which survive.

   Water carries many species to island shores. Tangled masses of roots
and trees flush out of coastal estuaries after every great rainstorm, inter-
twined with small animals, seeds, and whole plants. These natural rafts
may have been the main access to islands for immigrating species. Santa
Cruz Island presents a huge target, with the 23-mile-long axis of the
island broadside to prevailing currents. Island Foxes and Island Spotted
Skunks may have arrived by sea long ago.

   Motile animals also play an important role in populating islands.
Migratory and vagrant birds sometimes carry seeds on their feathers
and feet (and within their digestive tracts), only to preen them away on

an island perch. And many animals have immigrated to the island of their own volition. Fossils of Pygmy Mammoths, endemic to the Channel Islands, held paleontologists in suspense for decades as science tried to explain how these marooned elephants came to the islands. Ideas of a Pleistocene land connection were abandoned when geologists denied the possibility. The probable answer has surfaced only recently: the mammoths swam. People also arrived on their own volition, with the exception of shipwreck survivors. Chumash Indians have left evidence of occupation as old as 7,500 years. Their seafaring habits and active trading routes with mainland Chumash offered possible means of transportation for the island's two species of mice.

Ten plant communities are present, a remarkable variety for such a small area. Bishop Pine Forest occurs on three scattered, north-facing slopes, where persistent summer fogs provide moisture for survival. Coastal Sage Scrub perfumes the air around dry south-shore headlands and slopes. Most extensive is the Coastal Prairie community, covering about one-third of the island. In spring, Johnny Jump-ups, Common Fiddlenecks, Blue Dicks, and Goldfields splash color between clumps of Purple Needlegrass, Triple-awned Grass, and several species of alien annual grasses. A tiny succulent, Santa Cruz Island Live-forever, occupies a small patch of shoreline prairie and no other place on earth.

Other communities are dominated by island endemics. Greene's Live-forever, Island Alum Root, Santa Cruz Island Buckwheat, and a shrubby sunflower relative, Island Hazardia, cling to life in the Coastal Bluff community. Island Chaparral blankets many north-facing slopes, appearing like dark green velvet from a distance. Its dominant species, Island Manzanita and two endemic forms of California Lilac, are not found on the adjacent mainland. The dominant species of Island Ironwood Forest disappeared from the mainland three million years ago. Santa Cruz Island Ironwood, a tree wholly restricted to three of the Channel Islands, is in the Rose family and can reach 60 feet in height. Pure stands grow along geologic faults and contact zones. The high, rangy branches support dense clusters of distinctive dark green leaves and platter-sized heads of tiny cream-colored flowers.

Birds are by far the most common vertebrate animals on the island. Grasshopper Sparrows, Horned Larks, and Western Meadowlarks populate grasslands. Rufous-sided Towhees scratch at the duff beneath the chaparral, while endemic Orange-crowned Warblers whinny overhead. Acorn Woodpeckers and Northern Flickers riddle oak snags. Red-tailed Hawks and American Kestrels are abundant and patrol the skies. The Santa Cruz Island Scrub Jay ranges over the entire island but nowhere else in the world.

Endemic plants and animals are a common sight on Santa Cruz Island: forty-three species and subspecies of plants are found only on the Channel Islands (ten are restricted to Santa Cruz); nine of its birds are endemic subspecies; three of the reptiles and three or four of the mammals of Santa Cruz Island are not found on mainland California. They are all uniquely island products, strange and wonderful sights, certainly enough to fuel a novelist's imagination.

Islands over the world are filled with unusual forms of life. This island is rich in examples. Gigantic species of plants and animals abound. The endemic Santa Cruz Island Scrub Jay is twenty-five percent larger, and a much deeper blue, than its mainland counterpart. Other endemic birds, such as Orange-crowned Warblers and Rufous-sided Towhees, have oversized body parts, especially bills and feet. The Santa Cruz Island Buckwheat is the second largest species in this genus — the largest form is restricted to another island, Santa Catalina. Many island plants have assumed unusually large proportions, as their scientific names testify: Santa Cruz Island Buckwheat, *Eriogonum arborescens*; Island Alum Root, *Heuchera maxima*; and an island ceanothus, *Ceanothus arboreus*.

Other organisms have shrunk in their island isolation. The Island Fox, endemic to the Channel Islands, is the smallest fox species in North America, tipping the scales at a whopping four pounds. It is about one-third smaller than its closest relative, the Gray Fox. The Island Spotted Skunk is slightly smaller than its mainland counterpart. But the most remarkable dwarf was the Channel Islands Pygmy Mammoth, whose height ranged from 4.5 to 6 feet, as opposed to its closest relative, the Imperial Mammoth, whose twelve-foot height stands in tall contrast. A reconstructed skeleton on display at the Santa Barbara Museum of Natural History captures the imagination of schoolchildren. In fact, the last mammoth fossils discovered on Santa Cruz Island were found by two 12-year-old boys visiting the island in summer, 1985. Treasure Island.

Pirates had their day around the islands as well. The Cabrillo Expedition first sighted the Channel Islands in 1542, fifty years after Columbus's landing. For centuries the island remained practically unexplored by Europeans, but by the mid-1800s ranching on the island had begun. The first large-scale operation ran under the direction of Justinian Caire, whose Santa Cruz Island Company produced wine, wool, and other products for export. Many of the brick and adobe structures he built in the 1880s still stand today. In 1937, Edwin Stanton purchased most of the western portion of the island from the Caire family. In 1978, The Nature Conservancy, through a generous arrangement with Dr. Carey Stanton, Edwin Stanton's son, acquired over 12,000 acres of land and a conservation easement and future title to the remainder of the Santa Cruz Island Company property. Dr. Stanton passed away in December 1987, leaving the Conservancy in control of 90 percent of the island.

The Conservancy offers day trips to the island from April through November. Pelican Bay, the destination of most of these trips, is one of

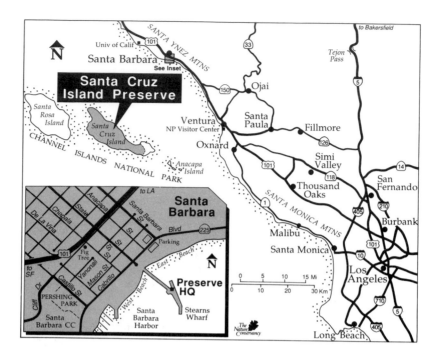

the most diverse areas of the island. Here five of the island's ten natural communities are clustered in a movie-backdrop setting: Coastal Bluff, Pine Forest, Chaparral, Riparian, and Grassland. The remains of the Pelican Bay Camp, where filming companies stayed and movie stars vacationed in the early part of the century, now serves as the trailhead for the Pelican Bay area.

An exciting part of an island visit is the channel crossing by charter vessel. Seabirds and marine mammals are abundant, and the two-and-a-half-hour crossing can be action-packed. As the boat slips past the island cliffs toward Pelican Bay, the swirling mists often present a mysterious air, one of a place where giant plants flourish and dwarf mammoths rest their bones.

—*Will Murray*

Will Murray is membership coordinator for the California Nature Conservancy. He served as preserve naturalist at the Santa Cruz Island preserve for five years.

Santa Cruz Island Checklist

SIZE

54,488 acres

SEASONAL HIGHLIGHTS

Wildflowers in spring; calm seas and migrating seabirds in fall.

WEATHER

Foggy and cool in early summer. Cool, clear, breezy afternoons midsummer. Warm, Indian-summer days in early autumn. Occasional severe southeast rainstorms in winter. Clear, windy days in spring. Summer maximums to 100 degrees, average mid-70s. Winter lows in 30s and 40s, highs in 60s and low 70s. Temperatures milder at the beaches, more extreme in the central valley. Average rainfall 20 inches.

ON-SITE FACILITIES

Steep, rough trails at Pelican Bay. Landing is by skiff; no docks available.

NEAREST OFF-SITE FACILITIES

23 miles across the Santa Barbara Channel in Santa Barbara or Ventura

EQUIPMENT

Layers of warm clothes for boat ride, comfortable clothes for hiking. Sturdy hiking shoes with good traction are essential. Binoculars. Food and water. Sun protection. Some people take seasickness medicine.

IMPORTANT

Hiking is over rugged terrain. You must be in good physical condition to visit this preserve.

TIME REQUIRED

Full day

TRANSPORTATION

Access to Santa Cruz Island is by either Conservancy-sponsored charter boat or private boat. To arrange for charter service, contact either Island Packers Company in Ventura at (805) 642-1393 or the Conservancy headquarters office listed below. Private yachts require a landing permit in advance (no permits are available at the island): Santa Cruz Island Company, P.O. Box 71940, Los Angeles, CA 90071-9208. Overnight visits are available by arrangement with Channel Island Adventures, 305 Durby Ave., Camarillo, CA 93010; (805) 987-1678.

The Nature Conservancy headquarters in Santa Barbara features exhibits about the Conservancy and Santa Cruz Island. The Nature Conservancy, 213 Stearns Wharf, Santa Barbara, CA 93101; (805) 962-9111. Open 10-4 daily. No charge. From Highway 101, take the Harbor exit. Follow Cabrillo Blvd. to Stearns Wharf at the foot of State Street. Parking is available in the city lot on Cabrillo Blvd. or on the wharf. The wharf is crowded on summer weekends.

TWENTY

Big Bear Valley
Glacial Legacy

NO PLACE in the entire continental United States has a higher concentration of unique species of rare plants than Big Bear Valley, located two hours east of Los Angeles in the San Bernardino Mountains. At least twenty-seven rare or endangered wildflowers thrive here on ice age soils. Sixteen of these are restricted in the world to the San Bernardino Mountains. Eleven others occur only here and in a few other locations in the mountains of Southern California. The site's geologic history, topography, and desert montane climate have conspired to create an amazing biological anomaly. Besides the unique endemics, over 300 other species of flowering plants bloom in the immediate vicinity. In some places, more than a dozen different species grow in a single square foot of ground. The federally endangered Slender-petaled Mustard, federally endangered Big Bear Checkerbloom, Eyestrain Monkeyflower, and extremely rare California Dandelion, Bear Valley Sandwort, and Munz's Hedgehog Cactus are only a few of the area's rarities that send rushes of color across the hills from late spring through early summer. Most are "belly plants"— delicate miniatures you have to get down at lizard level to appreciate.

But evolution here is not just limited to plants. At least two rare butterflies are known to exist within the preserve's boundaries. The Andrew's Marble and Little Blue depend on the rare plants for nectar and larval food. Other unique insects abound as well, including a wingless grasshopper whose natural coloring is the perfect camouflage; it blends right in with the surrounding clay soil and pebbles.

Unusual birds also congregate at the preserve. At least nine species of sparrows — including the rare Nevada Sage Sparrow — nest here. In winter, 25 to 30 Bald Eagles (the most in all of Southern California) perch along the shores of Big Bear and Baldwin lakes, while in fall, up to 3,000 Turkey Vultures pass through. Between 70,000 to 80,000 migrating

Bald Eagle

waterfowl light in fall, and in spring the meadows resound with the music of Western Meadowlark, Killdeer, and more.

Prior to the uplift of the northeast end of the San Bernardino Mountains (about 2.5 million years ago), Big Bear was covered by a huge Pleistocene lake that left a deep clay deposit over the area. Subsequent uplift has fragmented the deposit into a number of benchtop and valley clay lenses, ranging in elevation from approximately 6,500 to 7,500 feet.

At the end of the Ice Age, about 20,000 years ago, Mt. San Gorgonio was the southernmost peak on the north Pacific Coast to have held glaciers. It was not connected to the continental ice sheets, but was even then a glaciated island separated from the Sierra Nevada to the north by over a hundred miles. At that time Big Bear Valley, just ten miles north of San Gorgonio, was above timberline and was covered by an alpine flora of tufted, perennial herbs more typical of the modern Sierran alpine flora.

During a hot, dry climatic period about 10,000 years ago, the Mojave Desert expanded to the west, further isolating the San Bernardino

Mountains from the Sierra to the north. Conifer forests climbed higher in elevation with the more temperate climate, generally overtaking the alpine flora of Big Bear Valley, except on the clay soils of the ice age lake. The clay soils proved inhospitable to the trees, and, thus, the relict alpine flora has persisted on the treeless opening to this day. Frost heave pushes cobbles on the clay openings to the surface, hence the name "pebble plains." In some places, seasonal creeks flow through them, creating Alkali Vernal Meadows. In addition, limestone outcrops support rare endemic plants, such as Parish's Daisy. The three ecosystems are a showcase of evolution and speciation hard at work.

The site's unique flora has long attracted the interest of botanists. Pioneer botanist Samuel Bonsall Parish wrote about the area in 1917. Big Bear Valley came to the attention of The Nature Conservancy in 1980 when the California Natural Diversity Data Base noted that it contained extremely high concentrations of rare and endangered species. To help protect them, the Conservancy purchased an initial 97 acres at the north shore of Baldwin Lake. Since then, it has acquired additional parcels.

Baldwin Lake gets its name from "Lucky" Baldwin, a colorful character who made a fortune in the California gold rush. In 1874, Baldwin opened a gold mine on the lake's north shore. The area was once the home of Serrano Indians who gathered pinyon nuts in summer and fall and hunted ducks and Grizzly Bears. The gold rush spelled the end to both the Indians and the Grizzlies. Miners poured into the area, working the deposits on Gold Mountain, located on the west side of the present-day preserve. A boomtown sprang up nearby. Called Doble, it boasted three merchandise stores, two livery and feed stables, three restaurants, two hotels, several saloons, and a house of ill-repute. The boom was short-lived, however. In 1878, the local stamp mill burned down. Most of the mines soon played out. The only trace of Doble found today are tin cans and miners' graves.

Big Bear Valley is undergoing another boom today. Camping, boating, fishing, and skiing have turned it into a popular resort. On weekends and holidays the population swells to over 200,000. Vacation homes now crowd the shores of Big Bear Lake and threaten to engulf the entire valley. Biologists estimate that 2,000 to 3,000 acres of the area's original Vernal Meadow ecosystem has already been lost as the result of the creation of manmade Big Bear Lake and the ensuing housing development.

The Pebble Plains and Vernal Meadows that have survived support some of the most fascinating plants you'll find anywhere. Most of the area's wildflowers are genetic experiments that have developed an amazing plasticity and have adapted themselves to their environment in unique ways.

Big Bear Valley Preserve ▶

The region's valleys have an unusual east-west orientation that provides a range of microclimates to which different plants have responded in different ways. Take the endangered Big Bear Checkerbloom for example. At the west end of the valley annual rainfall averages 45 inches. The Big Bear Checkerbloom growing there sprouts large multiple-branching flower stalks. Yet just seven miles away at the east end of the valley, where precipitation averages only 15 inches a year, the plant sends up just a few small flower stalks.

Another plant displaying strange adaptation is the Ash-gray Paintbrush. One valley hybrid has twice the number of genes as either coastal or desert varieties. Like more common paintbrush plants, the Ash-gray has become a parasite. You can usually find it growing among silvery mats of Kennedy's Buckwheat—a rare plant parasitizing another rare plant.

April through July is the best time to enjoy the preserve's showy wildflower display, a time when the Pebble Plains and Vernal Meadows are covered by bright expanses of white, yellow, and violet. Yellow Violet and purple Parish's Rock-cress cover the plains in early April when snow still covers the surrounding peaks. In May, yellow Rayless Daisies dot the ground, and ephemeral annuals, such as the endemic Baldwin Lake Linanthus, make a brief appearance. Rose-and-white-striped Big Bear Checkerbloom add a dash of color. Ash-gray Paintbrush displays little yellow spikes, and fuzzy Rat-tails move in the wind. By June, the buckwheats bloom. Butterflies take nectar from the Slender-petaled Mustard. Tiny sprays of Bear Valley Sandwort mix with showy magenta bursts of the Munz's Hedgehog Cactus.

In the Vernal Meadows grow the rarest and most endangered species. Get down on your hands and knees and search for the aptly named Eyestrain Monkeyflower—the tiniest monkeyflower in the world. Use a hand lens to see the delicate one-tenth-inch pink corolla that grows on threadlike red stems. The endemic California Dandelion sports a lemon-yellow flower that is paler than its more common cousin. San Bernardino Butterweed and Yellow Clayflower stick to the saline clay pockets.

Summer is a good time to watch for birds. Williamson's and Red-breasted sapsuckers, Olive-sided Flycatcher, and Hermit Thrush are just a few of the season's highlights. Sora and Virginia Rail live in the bulrushes at the lake's edge, along with Great Blue and Black-crowned Night herons. Perhaps the best spectacle of the summer is the thousands of Eared Grebes that turn the lake into a floating nursery. You can spot chicks hitching rides on their parents' backs.

Fall brings wave after wave of migrating waterfowl—White Pelicans can make the lake look as if it's covered in snow. The prolific bird life attracts plenty of raptors, including Osprey, Swainson's Hawk, Ferruginous Hawk, and Black-shouldered Kite. The Baldwin Lake area is also home for the rare California Spotted Owl. Though still early in the

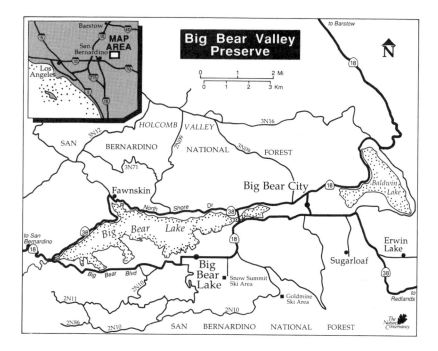

year for Bald Eagles, some begin arriving in late October and early November. There is plenty of mammal life, too. Mule Deer, Gray Fox, Bobcat, and Coyote congregate at the springs by the north shoreline.

To best enjoy the preserve's rare elements, take one of the guided natural history tours. Friends of the Big Bear Valley Preserve offer Bald Eagle tours by reservation during January and February and regularly scheduled wildflower walks from late spring through early summer. This organization works in concert with The Nature Conservancy and the U.S. Forest Service to preserve habitat in the valley.

Visit the Pebble Plains during the height of the wildflower display and you'll understand why Serrano Indians believed this was the birthplace of all wildflowers. According to legend, the Creator, Kukitat, was cremated on the site. So hot was his funeral pyre that it burned off all the trees and left the talus slopes. His ashes drifted throughout the high mountain valley. But each fragment of the old Kukitat blossomed into something new. Wildflowers appeared on the earth for the first time. From Kukitat's valley, they spread over the world.

Big Bear Valley Checklist

INFORMATION

For information and to make reservations for Bald Eagle and wildflower tours, contact the volunteers at P.O. Box 1418, Sugarloaf, CA 92386; (714) 866-4190.

SIZE

562 acres, in 15 separate parcels

SEASONAL HIGHLIGHTS

April through July wildflower display; January through February Bald Eagles.

WEATHER

Desert montane climate, dry with some rain in fall and snow in winter and spring. Strong winds.

ON-SITE FACILITIES

None

NEAREST OFF-SITE FACILITIES

In nearby community of Big Bear Lake

EQUIPMENT

good walking shoes
binoculars
magnifying glass
food and water
warm clothes in winter
snow chains for automobile in
    winter

TIME REQUIRED

3 to 4 hours

DIRECTIONS

From Los Angeles, take Highway 38 or 18 through the city of Big Bear Lake. Once in Big Bear Lake, take North Shore Drive (Hwy. 18) east until it begins a loop around Baldwin Lake. Parking is available in the gated area in front of the "Horse House" shack on the left (north) side of the highway for group tours, or one can turn left on Holcomb Valley Road (paved and marked) and proceed approximately one-half mile to a dirt parking area on the left at the end of the barbed wire fence at the Pacific Crest Trail crossing. The hike along the Pacific Crest Trail to the east (across the road several miles, one way) offers spectacular vistas over Baldwin Lake and the San Bernardino Mountains to the south, and the Mojave Desert to the north.

TWENTY-ONE

Big Morongo
Birdland

THE VISITOR's logbook at Big Morongo Preserve reads like a United Nations register. India, Switzerland, New Zealand, and Israel are a few of the countries represented. Apparently the word has spread all over the world: Big Morongo is big on birds. As many as 270 species have been spotted in this narrow, six-mile-long desert canyon two hours east of Los Angeles. Roger Tory Peterson included it in his list of places to visit in California during a North America record-tying "Big Day" in 1983. And for good reason; the stop netted him, among others, a Least Bell's Vireo, Vermilion Flycatcher, Black-chinned Sparrow, and Dusky Flycatcher.

Big Morongo boasts an astonishing number of unusual species. Counted among the more than 125 migrants are such rarities as Black-throated Blue Warbler, Tennessee Warbler, Red-eyed Vireo, American Redstart, and Ovenbird. It's one of a handful of special areas west of the Mississippi visited by birders searching for rare eastern migrants. Breeding birds number 72 species, including the Yellow-breasted Chat and Indigo Bunting. Compared with other Bureau of Land Management desert study areas, Big Morongo has three times the number of bird species.

Why such diversity and density? The answer lies in the site's location. The preserve is an ecotonal area between the Mojave Desert, the Colorado Desert, and the coast. This unusual blend of environments allows flora and fauna from all three habitats to coexist. The melange makes for some pretty strange bedfellows. Where else can you find a coast-loving Nuttall's Woodpecker nesting side by side with a desert-dwelling Ladder-backed Woodpecker?

Big Morongo Canyon is etched into the northwestern flank of the Little San Bernardino Mountains. The canyon was formed thousands of years ago when a plateau with two rivers running across it from north

Vermilion Flycatcher

to south dropped and became an abyss. The down-faulting generated so much friction and heat that the walls of the abyss were sealed, making it impervious to water. Some of the oldest rocks in California are exposed in the canyon. The heat and pressure transformed granite two billion years old into gneiss and schist. The two rivers continued draining into the abyss, creating a deep lake. They carried with them rocks, gravel, sand, and debris eroded from their courses as they carved Big Morongo Canyon and Little Morongo Canyon. The detritus ultimately buried the rivers and the lake and built the floor of Morongo Valley.

Moisture blown by winds from the Pacific precipitates as rain and snow on the slopes of nearby Mt. San Gorgonio, highest peak in Southern California. The runoff drains into subterranean rivers that continue to feed the underground lake. The overflow comes to the surface at the

◄ *Big Morongo Canyon Wildlife Preserve*

lower edges of the valley and forms two oases, one at Little Morongo Canyon, the other at the lower end of Big Morongo Canyon.

The lush, verdant oasis in Big Morongo is among the ten largest natural desert oases in the state, and it has the greatest variety of floral and faunal species of any of the twenty-two oases in the Mojave Desert. The year-round water supply nourishes one of the five largest tracts of cottonwood-willow habitat in the California desert, outside of the Colorado River.

Five distinct plant communities and at least 355 different types of plants thrive within the preserve's boundaries. A display of pressed specimens is available for viewing in a small trailer near the preserve manager's cabin.

The Creosote Bush Scrub community covers the hills and ridgetops above the creek. Mojave Yucca, Cat's Claw, Mormon Tea, and various species of cacti supply groundcover for such mammals as Coyote, Black-tailed Hare, and White-tailed Antelope Squirrel. Loggerhead Shrike preys on Side-blotched Lizard, Gilbert's Skink, and Desert Night Lizard, while covies of Gambel's Quail scurry single file through the Indigo Bush and Brittle-bushes. Northern Mockingbird and Scrub Jay shriek from California Juniper.

In the Desert Wash assemblage grows Buckhorn Cholla, Desert Catalpa, and Desert Mistletoe. Red Racer and Diamondback Rattlesnake lie in wait for Merriam's Kangaroo Rat and Long-tailed Pocket Mouse. Verdin, Phainopepla, and Cactus Wren flit among the mesquite.

Along the creek stands a healthy corridor of Riparian Woodland. The grove of Fremont Cottonwood, Red Willow, and Slender Willow provide nesting sites for Bewick's Wren, Common Bushtit, Cooper's Hawk, and Great Horned Owl. Gray Fox, Raccoon, and Ringtail are also riparian residents.

The Morongo Fault forces groundwater to the surface in a series of springs, resulting in over twenty acres of marsh. This wetland supports a Freshwater Marsh plant community: Cattail, Olney Bulrush, Yerba Mansa, and Watercress. Marsh Wren, Virginia Rail, Song Sparrow, and Common Yellowthroat feed and nest in this habitat. As water accumulates, it forms a stream that supports between two and three miles of riparian forest before becoming an open desert watercourse for four more miles.

The fifth plant community is not natural, but a cumulative result of longtime agricultural activities practiced in the area. The open fields were once planted with alfalfa. Now this plant community is labeled Desert Rural. The weedy annual plants are slowly being replaced by native Alkali Goldenbush, saltbush, willow, and Mesquite. Over these former fields soar Red-shouldered and Cooper's hawks and American Kestrels. Say's Phoebe feeds here as do Cassin's Kingbird, Western Meadowlark, and Brewer's Blackbird.

For centuries, Big Morongo Canyon was used by nomadic Indians as an easy route between high and low deserts. The oasis at the mouth of the canyon served as an ideal campsite. Water was available, game plentiful, and shelter in the form of caves was nearby. Five archaeological sites have been identified. Among the artifacts uncovered are fire rings, pottery shards, fragments of manos and metates, and grinding slicks and mortar holes. The Morongos, a powerful clan of the Serrano tribe, were the last Indians to live here. In 1864, a smallpox epidemic and severe drought forced them to move to a reservation near Banning.

The first white man to settle in Morongo Valley was Mark Bemis "Chuck" Warren. He established a ranch at the oasis in 1876, which became a stopping off point for travelers on the Big Morongo Canyon Road. The canyon lands passed from one rancher to the next until 1968, when 80 acres were sold as a partial gift to The Nature Conservancy by J. L. Covington. Soon after, 160 acres of adjacent land to the north was obtained by San Bernardino County to form the Big Morongo County Wildlife Preserve. The Bureau of Land Management recognized the area's outstanding ecological features and designated nearly 3,700 acres of ridge and canyon as an Area of Critical Environmental Concern in 1982. The Nature Conservancy is involved in the entire area through a lease with the Parks Department of San Bernardino County and a cooperative management agreement with the Bureau of Land Management.

Big Morongo Canyon has a desert climate with hot, dry summers and moderate winters. Rainfall averages eight inches a year. Though the preserve offers year-round birding, spring is surely the most popular time to visit. That's when colorful migrants stop by on their way back from South America.

A series of connecting nature trails loops through the preserve. A couple are boardwalks and can accommodate wheelchairs. The Cottonwood Trail leads from the information kiosk near the parking lot to the heart of the oasis. A strategically placed viewing platform has been built in the freshwater marsh. Here, shielded by eight-foot-high cattails, you can scan for birds. A pair of Yellow-breasted Chat nests nearby. Cottonwoods and willows spread overhead, and a different bird species seems to perch on every limb.

The brilliant Vermilion Flycatcher darts after passing insects, flits to low-hanging tree branches, and preens on perches. A Brown-crested Flycatcher launches itself from the towering cottonwoods. Like its scarlet-plumed cousin, it breeds no farther west than Big Morongo. They aren't the only flycatchers you'll find here. Other migrants include the Willow, Hammond's, Dusky, Gray, Western, Olive-sided, and Ash-throated species. Scissor-tailed Flycatcher and Greater Peewee have also been seen, but at this location both have to be considered accidentals.

Big Morongo is a good test for any birder. There are no fewer than

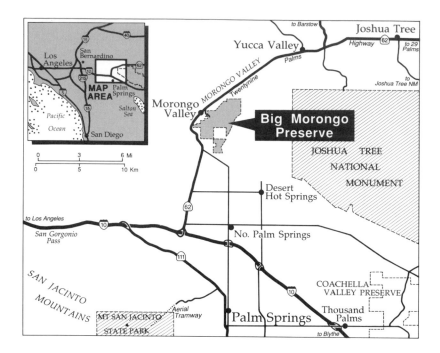

twenty-nine species of wood warblers to distinguish. It's uncommon for many of these species to occur in the west, rare for several, and downright bizarre for a few. Northern Parula and Cape May, Blackburnian, Bay-breasted, Red-faced, and Canada warblers are hardly common sights in California. Yet all have been spotted here at one time or another.

From the Cottonwood Trail you can catch the Willow Trail, which follows the creek as it winds beneath the multitiered greenery. This trail is guaranteed to strain your neck. A symphony of birdsong beckons you to look up into the overhanging branches. Don't forget to look down as well. Sora and Virginia Rail (once even a Black Rail) feed among the marsh plants as do thrashers, towhees, herons, and occasional ducks.

The Yucca Ridge Trail connects with the Willow Trail. Switchbacks up the canyon wall and along the ridgetop lead suddenly to the desert proper. Vaux's and White-throated swifts speed by, spiraling in the warm desert breezes. Black-chinned, Anna's, and Costa's hummingbirds sip nectar from the yellow flowers of Mesquite. Red-tailed Hawks freewheel on a rising thermal. While you are free of the trees, a look overhead during spring migration might provide the incongruous and exciting desert sight of a thousand White Pelicans or Double-crested Cormorants moving north for the summer.

The trail overlooks the fecund riparian corridor and gives you a bird's-eye view into all of the canyon's different habitats. Take a seat and you might get the surprise of your life. At dawn and dusk Desert Bighorn Sheep come down from the ridgetops during late summer to drink at the creek. Bobcat, Mountain Lion, and Black-tailed Mule Deer are also frequent visitors at the watering holes. At Big Morongo, there's no telling what you'll see next.

Big Morongo Checklist

INFORMATION

For information, contact the preserve manager at P.O. Box 780, Morongo Valley, CA 92256; (619) 363-7190.

SIZE

3,900 acres (80 under Conservancy ownership, 140 leased from San Bernardino County, and about 3,700 under cooperative management with the U.S. Bureau of Land Management)

SEASONAL HIGHLIGHTS

Year-round birding; bird migrations in in spring and fall.

WEATHER

Prepare for hot sun in summer and early fall and comfortably moderate but variable conditions from late fall to late spring.

ON-SITE FACILITIES

Information kiosk with interpretive displays, restrooms, nature trails — from short, level loops to long, hilly canyon hikes, picnic tables, drinking fountain

NEAREST OFF-SITE FACILITIES

One-quarter mile in town of Morongo Valley

EQUIPMENT

good walking shoes
binoculars
food and water
sun protection

TIME REQUIRED

Half day

DIRECTIONS

From Los Angeles, the preserve can be reached by traveling approximately 95 miles east on Interstate 10 to its junction with Highway 62. Travel 10½ miles north on 62. Turn right at East Drive (first road after the Morongo Preserve sign) and left into the preserve at the first hard-surface road. Trails begin from the parking lot kiosk into the riparian forest and extend the six-mile length of the canyon. The preserve parking lot is open from 7:30 A.M. to sunset daily.

Desert Bighorn Sheep

Ovis canadensis

*J*OHN MUIR called them "the bravest mountaineers." He was referring specifically to the Sierra Bighorn, but the description holds true for the Desert Bighorn subspecies as well.

Of California's bighorn sheep the Sierra is the rarest. Only 200 have survived a century-long assault by hungry gold miners, overhunting in general, and disease from domestic livestock. Their more common cousin, the Desert Bighorn, numbers about 3,700 in the state. They come in two varieties: the Nelson Bighorn, which lives in the desert mountain ranges in southeastern California, and the Peninsular Bighorn, which exists along the western edges of the desert from Palm Springs to Mexico. Herd sizes range from 700 in the San Gabriel Mountains north of Los Angeles to bands of 20 or fewer living in isolation among the Sheephole, Marble, and Chuckwalla mountains. Desert Bighorns frequent both the Coachella Valley and Big Morongo preserves.

Both the male and female bighorn grow horns that are never shed. You can tell an animal's age by the growth rings on the horns. The ewe's horns are flat, slightly curved, and measure only eight to ten inches long. The ram's horns are similar until he is two years old, when they begin to grow into a massive, round, full curl. The head and horns of an adult male can weigh more than 30 pounds. Some scientists suggest that the horns may have a thermoregulatory function, but as of yet the hypothesis is unconfirmed.

The color of the bighorn ranges from dark yellowish to grayish brown. The abdomen, rump, and insides of the legs are nearly pure white. They have keen vision and hearing. Bighorns prefer rough, high country where visibility is good and there is little competition from other grazing animals.

Most of the year adult rams move in separate bands from the ewes, younger rams, and lambs. But from September to December, they

Bighorn Sheep

gather together for the breeding season. Rams fight to determine who
will be the dominant animal, thus earning the right to do most of the
breeding.

The fights follow a pattern. Two males face off, glowering and snort-
ing. Finally, one raises its front hoof and taps the other on the chest. The
two rivals then turn and pace off a predetermined distance. Suddenly,
they reel and charge. As they come together—at a combined speed of 40
to 45 miles per hour—their upper bodies arch and their front hooves
leave the ground. Powerful muscles ripple down their thick necks and

across their massive shoulders. At the last moment they lower their horns and their foreheads smash together with a bone-chilling thud. They continue the brutal ritual until one declines to continue.

The females breed at 18 months and single lambs are born in 180 days. Weather plays the greatest limiting factor on lamb survival rate. Golden Eagles prey on the young bighorns, as do Mountain Lions and Coyotes.

TWENTY-TWO

Coachella Valley

Island in a Sea of Sand

WHEN CECIL B. deMille needed an oasis to serve as backdrop for his film *King of Kings*, he had to search no farther than a hundred miles east of Hollywood. Just outside of Palm Springs stands Thousand Palms, one of the largest and most breathtaking groves of native fan palms in the entire Southwest. Here in the shade of rustling fronds bubble pools of crystal clear water freed by earthquake faults.

A watery island in a sea of sand, this lush and fecund wellspring provides refuge for more than 130 species of plants and 180 species of animals. It is the heart of a unique and very delicate 13,000-acre blow-sand ecosystem, the largest remnant of its kind in the state, now protected as the Coachella Valley Preserve.

Strange things happen in the desert. Visions float like dreams on the horizon. Rivers of sand turn into torrents in a flash. Winds send boulders the size of refrigerators skidding across flats of alkali. But surely one of the most unusual incidents ever to occur in the desert was the creation of this preserve—living proof that sometimes cooperation, not litigation, can be nature's best defense.

Lumping the event with other natural phenomena of the arid Southwest may be stretching literary license a bit thin, but it really does fall into the category of amazing stories, especially considering how bitter desert land-use conflicts have been. This time, however, nine cities, a county, several state and federal agencies, an Indian tribe, the real estate industry, builders, resource experts, wildlife biologists, and conservationists figured out a way to set aside their differences, agree on a single course of action, and carry it out.

The common ground this disparate group found centered on a chunk of priceless real estate inhabited by *Uma inornata*, a secretive little reptile more commonly known as the Coachella Valley Fringe-toed Lizard.

A creature of antiquity, the lizard dwells exclusively on deposits of blow-sand of exacting particle size and shape. Blow-sands are fine silts that have been flushed out of the mountains by flash floods, picked up by unidirectional winds, and carried some distance downwind, where they form dunes and hummocks. The habitat is spartan. On summer days the surface sizzles at temperatures of up to 180 degrees. Protective rocks and shading shrubs are essentially nonexistent. Rain falls, but rarely.

Few vertebrates can survive such hostile terrain, yet *Uma* turns adversity to advantage. A marvel of adaptation, the fringe-toed lizard can submerge into sand and move through it to escape the intense heat and predators.

In 1972, Wilbur "Bill" Mayhew, a professor of zoology at nearby UC Riverside, discovered that population levels of the fringe-toed lizard were in serious decline. Habitat loss was clearly to blame. More than half of the original 267 square miles available to the lizard had been destroyed. Worse, another 2.5 square miles of remaining habitat was being converted each year. At that rate, the Coachella Valley would reach build-out by the turn of the century.

Mayhew quickly went to work to save what was left of the beleaguered ecosystem. He figured his best chance was to get the fringe-toed listed under the Endangered Species Act so state and federal money could be made available for habitat acquisition. It was an uphill battle, but after a decade of perseverance, Mayhew finally succeeded.

Official designation as a "threatened" species meant that developers would be breaking the law if they destroyed lizard habitat. Hoping to keep future projects from being stalled by protracted legal battles, developers finally decided to cooperate. A meeting was held in June 1983 between various government officials, developers, and conservationists.

The meeting began like a United Nations debate — as many points of view as participants — but eventually the multi-interest group discovered it had a common goal. All sought an equitable resolution. The answer was a seldom-used amendment to the Endangered Species Act. Section 10(a) gives the Secretary of the Interior authority to resolve such conflicts by granting a permit to allow incidental taking of a protected species, conditioned on the implementation of a specific set of conservation measures, otherwise known as a Habitat Conservation Plan.

The most logical conservation plan, the Coachella Valley group concluded, was Mayhew's original concept of a preserve. A compromise was worked out so developers would get the "incidental take" permit in exchange for paying mitigation fees, to be used to help finance a preserve. It was precedent setting.

In about as much time as it takes to construct an 18-hole course in this golf capital of the world, the group pieced together some forty contiguous parcels of deeded property and purchased them for a preserve. The effort that went into appraising each property, negotiating a price, and securing financing was enough to make even the most ambitious real estate broker cringe.

The Nature Conservancy primed the pump by pledging $2 million, a donation from the Richard King Mellon Foundation. In April 1984 it bought 2,000 acres, including the achingly beautiful Thousand Palms Oasis. The Bureau of Land Management then agreed to $5 million in land exchanges, and the California Department of Fish and Game contributed another $2 million. Developers agreed to pay $600 per acre over eight years for a total of $7 million in mitigation fees, while Congress chipped in a final $10 million. The $25 million price tag reportedly made it the most expensive single-species conservation project ever attempted.

In truth, much more than just the fringe-toed lizard benefits from the creation of the Coachella Valley Preserve. Four other rare species dwell here, as do numerous other unusual plants and animals. Phainopepla, Hooded Oriole, Cactus Wren, Black Phoebe, and Verdin are just a few of the twenty-five bird species that nest at the oasis. Bobcats are a common sight, even in broad daylight.

Willis Palms, Indian Palms, and Hidden Palms are the other oases within the preserve's boundaries. Together they support 1,200 native California Fan Palms, the second largest concentration of native palms in the state. The shaded waters, fed by continuously flowing springs seeping along the San Andreas Fault, have also provided humans with relief from the harsh desert sands for more than 600 years.

The Cahuilla Indians found shelter here, gathering edibles from Mesquite, Agave, and Yucca, and hunting resident Bighorn Sheep, Black-tailed Mule Deer, Pronghorn, rodents, and rabbits. Later, trappers, prospectors, and homesteaders came. In 1906, an early California rancher, Louis Wilhelm, gave "Alkali Al" Thornberg two mules and a buckboard in trade for the oasis and surrounding eighty acres. Wilhelm built a two-room house out of palm wood near the oasis's pools. Today it serves as the preserve's information center.

In sharp contrast to the lush oasis is the surrounding desert. Its floor is composed of alluvial fans and isolated terraces of desert pavement dissected by wash areas in the north and extensive aeolian sand fields and dunes in the south. The largest alluvial fan begins at the southern edge of the Indio Hills at the mouth of Thousand Palms Canyon. Here rocks and sands eroded from the Little San Bernardino Mountains create a coarse, cobblestone surface that is broken by a network of narrow, sandy washes. The persistent westerly winds in the Coachella Valley move the finer particles and sands from the southern portion of this fan into the ever-changing blow-sand fields. This cycle of moving and blowing sand continually regenerates the desert system, providing habitat for an extraordinary diversity of life.

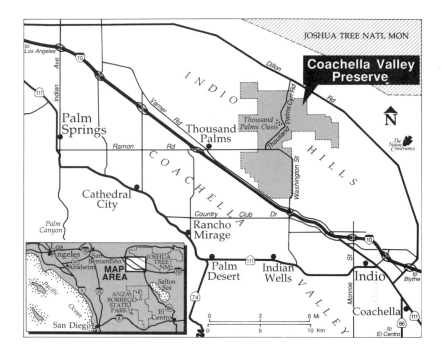

Given the current pace of desert development, the preserve one day will be to Coachella Valley what Central Park is to New York.

The best way to explore the preserve is to take the self-guided interpretive trail, an easy, mile-long loop that begins at the Palm House and winds through the lush groves and along a chain of pools that gleam like pearls. Look closely in the water and you'll spy schools of small fish. Watch for birds feeding in the Encelia, Smoke Trees, and Creosote Bushes. If you're lucky, you might even spot a Flat-tailed Horned Lizard scuttling across the sand, or a fringe-toed diving into a dune.

Spring, fall, and winter are the best seasons to visit—summer temperatures reach 120 degrees. Dawn and dusk provide the most to see. Wildlife are most active in the cooler hours. During these times, the desert sun brushes the sky with colors and the ocher hills reflect the changing palette. Wind rustles the palm fronds, and on especially breezy days, if you close your eyes, the noise sounds like crashing surf.

◄ *Coachella Valley Preserve*

Coachella Valley Checklist

The preserve is open every day from sunrise to sunset. Individuals and groups are welcome. For more information, contact the preserve manager at P.O. Box 188, Thousand Palms, CA 92276; (619) 323-1234.

SIZE

13,000 acres

SEASONAL HIGHLIGHTS

Wildflowers in spring; migratory birds in spring and fall.

WEATHER

Desert climate, with an annual rainfall of 3 inches. Temperatures can climb to 100 degrees in July and fall to 39 degrees in January.

ON–SITE FACILITIES

Visitor Center, picnic tables, self–guided interpretive trail.

NEAREST OFF–SITE FACILITIES

10 miles east in Palm Springs

EQUIPMENT

good walking shoes
binoculars
food and ample water
hat and sun protection
seasonally appropriate clothing

TIME REQUIRED

Half day

DIRECTIONS

Coachella Valley Preserve is located in Riverside County, roughly ten miles east of Palm Springs. From Interstate 10, exit on Ramon Road and drive east to Thousand Palms Canyon Drive. Turn left (north), drive two miles to the preserve's entrance on left (look for red wagon wheels). Park in designated area and walk 100 yards to the Visitor Center in the Palm House.

Coachella Valley Fringe-toed Lizard

Uma inornata

ALSO KNOWN as the "sand swimmer," the Coachella Valley Fringe-toed Lizard lives exclusively in blow-sand fields. A marvel when it comes to adaptation, the eight-to ten-inch lizard can literally swim through sand to escape the searing heat and such fearsome predators as Greater Roadrunners, whipsnakes, Burrowing Owls, and Loggerhead Shrikes.

From its head right down to its toes, this lizard is a shining example of nature's talent for ingenious engineering. It has evolved a sharp-edged jaw and chisel-shaped skull so it can dive into sand dunes. Smooth, round scales on the skin reduce friction as it "swims," and fringes — enlarged scales, really — on hind toes give it traction and propel it underground. The lower jaw fits snugly into the overlapping upper jaw, and the oval nostril openings are adjustable, possessing a U-shaped trap — wondrous adaptations that allow the lizard to breathe air between grains without inhaling the sand. Flaps of fringed skin work as a kind of built-in ear muffler to protect external openings during dives, and overlapping eyelids also keep out grit.

Acutely sensitive to light, sound, and vibrations while underground, the sand swimmer can easily detect the slightest movement of small insects overhead. A third eye, or parietal eye, is located on the top of its head and exhibits well-developed lens- and retina-like structures. Herpetologists say the eye monitors the amount of solar radiation the animal receives, triggering a release of chemical signals to the brain so the lizard will know when to come in out of the sun to avoid overheating. The parietal eye is still something of a scientific mystery, but researchers are exploring whether its properties might be useful in developing a cure for such human mental disorders as schizophrenia.

Like most reptiles of southwestern desert regions, the fringe-toed spends winter months in hibernation. Come November it simply buries

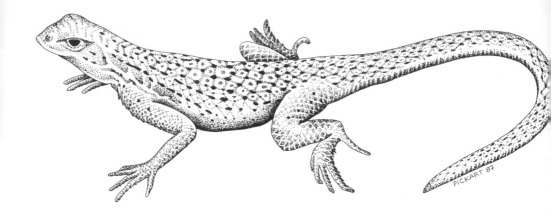

Coachella Valley Fringe-toed Lizard

itself in the sand and snoozes away until the first warm days of February bring it scratching back to the surface. May is courtship time. Males begin a tireless round of ritualistic push-ups that would make a high school phys-ed coach proud. These zealous exercises lure females who find the macho bobbings sexually irresistible. Spectators soon become participants. Typically, a male grabs the skin of a female's neck in his jaws, prods her with his legs to make her flip her tail, and inserts one of his two hemipenes into her cloaca. A few weeks later she digs a burrow and deposits her eggs. Hatchlings usually appear about four to eight weeks later. No one knows for sure exactly how long incubation takes.

Two other species of the genus *Uma* are found in the United States: the Mojave Fringe-toed Lizard (*U. scoparia*) and the Colorado Desert Fringe-toed Lizard (*U. notata*). Another pair live south of the border in the Chihuahuan Desert: *U. exsul* and *U. paraphygas*. An unusually mobile ecosystem is suspected to be the primary cause for the now separate lineages. Fringe-toeds are confined to sand dune systems pushed slowly along by the wind over thousands of years. Occasionally systems separate, isolating lizard populations. Apparently, some of these separated groups found their own genetic course and became reproductively independent. As a group, fringe-toeds appear to be thriving, but not the Coachella Valley species. It had the misfortune of riding a dune straight into what has become one of the most desirable communities in the country.

TWENTY-THREE

Santa Rosa Plateau

Old California

ROLLING GRASSLAND, old Engelmann Oaks, freshwater tenajas, and an historic adobe at the Santa Rosa Plateau Preserve bespeak an age of county-sized Mexican land grants and gracious haciendas. Here, just a few miles from the front line of Riverside's burgeoning population, time seems to have stood still. In the drowsy sun, one can easily imagine vaqueros resplendent in charro suits riding across the fields.

Little has changed at this former ranch since the early Mission days. Most of its resident flora and fauna still exist. Few other places in Southern California can make that claim. The preserve provides a home for at least 588 species of vascular plants, 144 species of birds, 80 species of lichens, and 26 species of fungi. Three uncommon native plant communities are protected: Engelmann Oak Woodland, Upland Native Bunchgrass Prairie, and Vernal Pool. Endangered species include California Orcutt Grass, San Diego Button-celery, Thread-leaf Brodiaea, San Miguel Savory, Stephens' Kangaroo Rat, Meadowfoam, and Orcutt's Brodiaea.

The Santa Rosa Plateau lies at the southern end of the Santa Ana Mountains. Several crumbling mesas cap the plateau, and its topography ranges to 2,200 feet elevation. At one time, the area comprised gently rolling alluvial land underlain by older granite and metamorphic formations. During a period of comparatively undramatic volcanism, lava flowed from surface vents and covered the plains. As time passed, the softer or thinner areas eroded away, leaving mesas protected by basalt caps. Ultimately, these too will erode away.

The breakdown of basalt creates an extremely expansive soil that allows very little water loss through seepage. Rainwater from winter storms collects in the low spots until it evaporates. These depressions are called vernal pools. Few remain in Southern California today. In River-

side County, only fourteen vernal pools survive; thirteen are protected on the Santa Rosa Plateau.

The pools occur on three of the plateau's flat-topped mesas — four on Mesa de Colorado, one on Mesa de la Punta, and the remaining eight on Mesa de Burro. At over thirty acres, the Mesa de Colorado pool is one of the largest in the state. Rains fill it with water from December through mid-May. The rest of the year it is completely dry. As the water recedes in spring, yellow Goldfields and sky-blue Downingia cover its banks. Several endangered plants depend on this pool for survival. All the pools are visited in winter by ducks, geese, grebes, gulls, Greater Yellowlegs, Whimbrels, Least Sandpipers, and Long-billed Dowitchers.

Several creeks also flow through the preserve. Though they dry up during the rainless summer months, many deep holes in the beds contain water year-round. Some are springfed. These are called tenajas, Spanish for "tanks," and in rancho times were used as watering holes for livestock. The tenajas serve as critical habitat for reptiles and amphibians, such as the Western Pond Turtle and Red-legged Frog. Dozens of bird species nest in the surrounding riparian growth made up of Western Sycamore and Red Willow.

Surely the most striking tree on the preserve is the Engelmann Oak. Fossil remains indicate this rare species was once widespread throughout the western United States. Now it ranges only from Santa Barbara to San Diego. The trees at Santa Rosa Plateau compose one of the last remaining viable stands in the state. Elsewhere, the oaks have been reduced to just a few aging specimens apparently incapable of regeneration.

The oak is named for Dr. George Engelmann, a German-born physician who conducted botanical explorations in this country during the 1800s. In appearance, the tree differs markedly from the more common Coast Live Oak, which also grows in abundance on the preserve. The Engelmann Oak is more gnarled and angular, has a checkered or fissured trunk, grayish leaves, and short, round acorns. The Coast Live Oak looks fuller. The bark is smoother, leaves are shiny green with small teeth, and the acorns are longer and more slender. Engelmanns usually grow on high, dry ground. Coast Live Oaks prefer lower, wetter spots.

Upland Native Bunchgrass Prairie, another rare plant community here, is the largest expanse of its type in all of Southern California. Such perennials as Purple Needlegrass and Malpais Bluegrass help the prairie retain some of its pristine character, despite the invasion of Mediterranean annual grasses and forbs. Showy native wildflowers bloom among the grasses following winter rains. Some of the more common flowering species are Blue Dicks, Johnny Jump-up, Mariposa Lily, lupine, Checkerbloom, and Shooting Star.

◄ *Santa Rosa Plateau Preserve*

Patches of chaparral also cover the preserve. Scrub Oak, Toyon, Chamise, and manzanita mix with Black Sage, White Sage, and Red-berry to create perfect habitat for such birds as California Thrasher, Common Bushtit, California Quail, Greater Roadrunner, and Rufous-sided Towhee.

For 6,000 years Indians of the Shoshonean language group used the area to hunt for Black-tailed Mule Deer, rabbits, and other wildlife, as well as to gather acorns during the fall. Their presence is evident from mortar holes in the outcroppings of granite, made by grinding acorns into meal with rock pestles. Shallow depressions in rock surfaces — called metates — were used to grind smaller seeds with hand-held manos. Two areas have been identified as religious sites — one for men, the other for women.

In 1846 the land became part of a 47,000-acre Mexican land grant, Rancho Santa Rosa, given to Juan Moreno by Governor Pio Pico. Moreno constructed several adobe buildings and grazed cattle in the grassland fields. The land changed hands several times over the years until 1904 when the Vail family took title. They held the land for sixty years, then sold it to the Kaiser Corp in 1964. To protect the rare natural values of this important part of California's heritage, the Conservancy acquired 3,100 acres and established the Santa Rosa Plateau Preserve on January 1, 1984.

Two miles down the old road from the parking area is the preserve headquarters, an old adobe that dates back to the mid to late 1800s. It was built by the rancho's second owners, the Machados, and was later used as a jail for drunken vaqueros. The oaks giving shade to the adobe are at least 300 years old. A noisy colony of Acorn Woodpeckers can be heard pecking incessantly at the bark. Lewis's, Nuttall's, and Downy woodpeckers also live on the preserve, as well as Yellow-bellied and Red-breasted sapsuckers and Northern Flickers. Placed around the field in front of the adobe are three nesting boxes used by Western Bluebirds. Black-shouldered Kites and Red-shouldered Hawks soar over the field. Inside the cool adobe are interpretive displays of the preserve's various natural communities. Here you can pick up brochures and maps to the two self-guided nature trails.

The Engelmann Oak Woodland Trail is a level hike that takes less than an hour at a leisurely pace. The trail goes through stands of Engelmann and Coast Live oaks, near an Indian occupation site, alongside a creek, by a tenaja, through a field of grassland, and to a dike of old meta-morphic rock that has intruded into a crack in the existing softer rock. In the stand of Western Sycamores and willows by the creek, watch for nesting Black Phoebes, Lesser Goldfinches, and Red-winged Black-birds. The rotting trunks of the old sycamores make great homes for cavity dwellers. If you approach the tenaja quietly, you might spot Western Pond Turtles sunning themselves in the middle of the pond on rocks and logs.

The Vernal Pool and Overlook Trail is a level but rocky walk. The condition of the trail varies considerably with the season; during wet times, a complete circuit could be impossible due to the water level of the pools or very sticky mud. Spring is the best time to take it. The trail leads across the Mesa de Colorado to two vernal pools. You'll pass patches of Prickly Pear Cactus, a plant that provides both food and shelter for a variety of small birds and rodents. In late spring and summer it bears large yellow or salmon flowers, followed by reddish fruit called, strangely enough, "tunas."

As you cross the mesa, you'll be able to see a good example of an Engelmann Oak community. Be careful. In summer, the rocks near the trees provide shelter for Red Diamond and Western rattlesnakes. The creek that flows near the trail drains water from the mesa and is festooned in spring with bright yellow-petaled California Buttercups.

Be quiet as you approach the vernal pool. An abundance of waterfowl uses it regularly during the wet season. Green-winged and Cinammon teals, Mallard, Northern Pintail, Northern Shoveler, and Ring-necked Duck are just a few species you can expect to see. Near the pool are curious piles of rock. The origin of the piles remains a mystery, but speculation is they were used by Indians as duck blinds. Pacific Tree Frogs croak among them.

Step out on the flat rocks at the edge of the pool and look down. A variety of plants sends up green shoots with the first rains. They bloom and set seeds before the summer dry period. Two of the rarest plants in California grow in this pool: California Orcutt Grass and San Diego Button-celery. Both grow underwater during winter and spring and bloom when all the water has evaporated, usually in late May or early June.

From the Vernal Pool Trail take a side loop on the Overlook Trail across to the edge of the mesa. From here, look southwest, and, on a clear day, you can see all the way to Oceanside Harbor eighteen miles away on the Pacific coast. Turn around for a view of the entire preserve. The wind sends ripples across fields of Purple Needlegrass. Rare plants spring to life around the edges of vernal pools. Centuries-old Engelmann Oaks stand majestically. And across the preserve, Golden Eagles launch themselves from the cliffs of Mesa de Burro to soar high over this relic of old California.

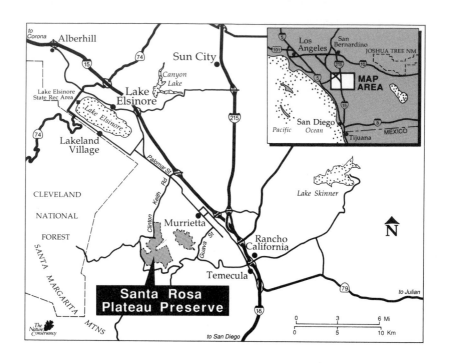

Santa Rosa Plateau Checklist

INFORMATION

Self-guided trails are available to visitors on a drop-in basis. Guided tours led by a trained docent are available by advanced arrangements to schools and other groups. For more information, contact the preserve manager at: 22115 Tenaja Road, Murrieta, CA 92362; (714) 677-6951.

SIZE

3,100 acres

SEASONAL HIGHLIGHTS

Bird migrations in spring and fall; spring wildflower display through April.

WEATHER

Moderated by marine influence

ON-SITE FACILITIES

Two self-guided nature trails, information kiosk, Visitor Center and picnic tables are a two-mile hike at preserve headquarters

NEAREST OFF-SITE FACILITIES

5 miles away in Murrieta

EQUIPMENT

good walking shoes
binoculars
food and water
magnifying glass
sun protection

TIME REQUIRED

All day

DIRECTIONS

Preserve is located off Interstate 15, 40 miles south of the city of Riverside. Exit Clinton Keith Road at Murrieta. Drive west 5 miles to preserve entrance at Tenaja Road (locked gate).

Species List

The California Nature Conservancy preserves provide habitat for thousands of species of plants and animals. Those species discussed in this guide are listed below with their scientific names.

Agave	*Agave deserti*
Alder, White	*Alnus rhombifolia*
Allocarya, Scribe	*Allocarya scripta*
Alum Root, Island	*Heuchera maxima*
Asellid, California Eyed	*Caecidotia tomalensis*
Ash, Oregon	*Fraxinus latifolia*
Aster, Mojave	*Machaeranthera tortifolia*
Avocet, American	*Recurvirostra americana*
Azolla	*Azolla filiculoides*
Badger	*Taxidea taxus*
Barley, Alkali	*Hordeum depressum*
Hare	*H. leporinum*
Bay, California	*Umbellularia californica*
Bear, Black	*Ursus americanus*
Grizzly	*U. chelan*
Bearberry	*Arctostaphylos uva-ursi*
Beaver	*Castor canadensis*
Beetle, Delta Green Ground	*Elaphrus viridus*
Bittern, American	*Botaurus lentiginosus*
Blackberry, California	*Rubus vitifolius*
Himalayan	*R. procerus*
Blackbird, Brewer's	*Euphagus cyanocephalus*
Red-winged	*Agelaius phoeniceus*
Tri-colored	*A. tricolor*
Yellow-headed	*Xanthocephalus xanthocephalus*

Bladderwort	*Utricularia gibba*
	U. vulgaris
Blazing Star	*Mentzelia lindleyi*
Blennosperma	*Blennosperma nanum*
Blue Dicks	*Dichelostemma pulchra*
Bluebird, Western	*Sialia mexicana*
Blue-eyed Grass	*Sisyrinchium bellum*
Bluegrass, Annual	*Poa annua*
Malpais	*P. scabrella*
Pacific	*P. gracillima*
Pine	*P. scabrella*
Bobcat	*Lynx rufous*
Brittle-bush	*Encelia farinosa*
Brodiaea, Orcutt's	*Brodiaea orcuttii*
Thread-leaf	*B. filifolia*
Brome, Red	*Bromus rubens*
Ripgut	*B. diandrus*
Buckeye, California	*Aesculus californica*
Buckwheat, California	*Eriogonum fasciculatum*
Coast	*E. latifolium*
Cottony	*E. gossypinum*
Ione	*E. apricum*
Kennedy's	*E. kennedyi*
Santa Cruz Island	*E. arborescens*
Tiburon	*E. caninum*
Bulrush, Olney	*Scirpus olneyi*
Bunting, Indigo	*Passerina cyanea*
Lark	*Calamospiza melanocorys*
Lazuli	*Passerina amoena*
Burrobush	*Franseria dumosa*
Bushtit, Common	*Psaltriparus minimus*
Butter-and-Eggs	*Orthocarpus erianthus*
Buttercup, California	*Ranunculus californicus*
Lobb's	*R. lobbii*
Butterfly, Andrew's Marble	*Euchloe hyantis andrewsii*
Buckeye	*Junonia caenia*
California Sister	*Adelpha bredowi*
Eunus Skipper	*Pseudocopaeodes eunus*
Little Blue	*Philotes enoples*
Monarch	*Danaus plexippus*
Mourning Cloak	*Numphalis antiopa*
San Emigdio Blue	*Plebulina emigdionis*
Tiger Swallowtail	*Papilo rutulus*
Veined White	*Artogeia napi veinosa*

Xerces Blue	*Glaucopsyche xerces*
Butterweed, San Bernardino	*Senecio bernardinus*
Buttonbush	*Cephalanthus occidentalis*
Button-celery, San Diego	*Eryngium aristulatum parishii*
Button-willow	*Cephalanthus occidentalis*
Cactus, Beavertail	*Opuntia basilaris*
Munz's Hedgehog	*Echinocereus munzii*
Prickly Pear	*Opuntia littoralis*
Calycadenia, Fremont's	*Calycadenia fremontii*
Canvasback	*Aythya valisineria*
Cat's Claw	*Acacia greggii*
Catalpa, Desert	*Chilopsis linearis*
Cattail	*Typha spp.*
Ceanothus	*Ceanothus arboreus*
Island	*C. megacarpus insularis*
Cedar, Incense	*Calocedrus decurrens*
Celery, Wild	*Apiastrum angustifolium*
Chamise	*Adenostoma fasciculatum*
Char, Dolly Varden	*Salvelinus confluentus*
Chat, Yellow-breasted	*Icteria virens*
Checkerbloom	*Sidalcea malvaeflora*
Cheese Brush	*Hymenoclea salsola*
Chia	*Salvia columbariae*
Chickadee, Chestnut-backed	*Parus rufescens*
Chinquapin, Giant	*Castanopsis chrysophylla*
Cholla, Buckhorn	*Opuntia acanthocarpa*
Chukar	*Alectoris chukar*
Clayfower, Yellow	*Haplopappus uniflorus gossypinus*
Clematis	*Clematis ligusticifolia*
Clover, Elk's	*Aralia californica*
Showy Indian	*Trifolium amoenum*
Coffeberry, California	*Rhamnus californica*
Condor, California	*Gymnogyps californicus*
Cone Flower, California	*Anemopsis californica*
Coot, American	*Fulica americana*
Coral-root, Spotted	*Corallorhiza maculata*
Cormorant, Double-crested	*Phalacrocorax auritus*
Cottontail, Desert	*Sylvilagus audobonii*
Cottonwood, Fremont	*Populus fremontii*
Coyote	*Canis latrans*
Coyote Brush	*Baccharis pilularis*
Coyote Melon	*Cucurbita foetidissima*
Crab, Lined Shore	*Pachygrapsus crassipes*
Crane, Sandhill	*Grus canadensis*

Whooping	*G. americana*
Creambush	*Holodiscus discolor*
Creeper, Brown	*Certhia americana*
Creosote Bush	*Larrea tridentata*
Crossbill, Red	*Loxia curvirostra*
Crow, American	*Corvus brachyrhynchos*
Cuckoo, Yellow-billed	*Coccyzus americanus*
Cucumber, Wild	*Marah macrocarpa*
Curlew, Long-billed	*Numenius americanus*
Daisy, Parish's	*Erigeron parishii*
Rayless	*E. aphanactis*
Seaside	*E. maritima*
Dandelion, California	*Taraxacum californicum*
Deer, Black-tailed Mule	*Odocoileus hemionus*
Deer Brush	*Ceanothus integerrimus*
Desert Candle	*Caulanthus inflatus*
Desert-dandelion	*Malacothrix glabrata*
Desert Thorn, Anderson	*Lycium andersonii*
Dipper, American	*Cinclus mexicanus*
Dodder, Howell's	*Cuscuta howelliana*
Dogwood, Pacific	*Cornus nuttallii*
Douglas-fir	*Pseudotsuga menziesii*
Dove, Mourning	*Zenaida macroura*
Dowitcher, Long-billed	*Limnodromus scolopaceus*
Short-billed	*L. griseus*
Downingia	*Downingia bella D. bicornuta*
Duck, Ring-necked	*Aythya collaris*
Ruddy	*Oxyura jamaicensis*
Wood	*Aix sponsa*
Duckweed	*Lemna sp.*
Eagle, Bald	*Haliaeetus leucocephalus*
Golden	*Aquila chrysaetos*
Eatonella, Congdon's	*Eatonella congdonii*
Egret, Great	*Casmerodius albus*
Elder, Box	*Acer negundo californicum*
Elderberry	*Sambucus mexicana*
Elk, Tule	*Cervus nannodes*
Encelia	*Encelia californica*
Eupatory, Shasta	*Eupatorium shastense*
Fairy Bells	*Disporum oreganum*
Falcon, Peregrine	*Falco peregrinus*
Prairie	*F. mexicanus*
Fern, Bracken	*Pteridium aquilinum*
Five-finger	*Adiantum pedatum*

Maiden-hair	*A. jordannii*
Polypody	*Polypodium sp.*
Shield	*Polystichum californicum*
Sword	*P. munitum*
Venus-hair	*Adiantum capillus-veneris*
Wood	*Dryopteris arguta*
Fescue, Few-flowered	*Festuca reflexa*
Foxtail	*F. megaleura*
Small	*F. microstachys*
Fiddleneck, Common	*Amsinckia intermedia*
Forked	*A. furcata*
Filaree, Red-stem	*Erodium cicutarium*
Fir, Grand	*Abies grandis*
Santa Lucia	*A. bracteala*
White	*A. concolor*
Fisher	*Martes pennanti*
Flax, Marin Dwarf	*Hesperolinon congestum*
Flicker, Northern	*Colaptes auratus*
Flycatcher, Ash-throated	*Myriarchus cinerascens*
Brown-crested	*M. tyrannulus*
Dusky	*Empidonax oberholseri*
Gray	*E. wrightii*
Hammond's	*E. hammondii*
Olive-sided	*Contopus borealis*
Scissor-tailed	*Tyrannus forficatus*
Vermilion	*Pyrocephalus rubinus*
Western	*Empidonax difficilis*
Willow	*E. traillii*
Fox, Gray	*Urocyon cinereoargentus*
Island	*U. littoralis*
San Joaquin Kit	*Vulpes macrotis mutica*
Foxtail, Pacific Meadow	*Alopecurus saccatus*
Frog, Pacific Tree	*Hyla regilla*
Red-legged	*Rana aurora*
Fuchsia, California	*Zauschneria californica*
Gadwall	*Anas strepera*
Gilia, Bird's-eye	*Gilia tricolor*
Godwit, Marbled	*Limosa fedoa*
Gold Nuggets	*Calochortus luteus*
Goldenbush, Alkali	*Haplopappus linearifolius*
Goldenhead	*Acamptopappus sphaerocephalus*
Goldfields	*Lasthenia chrysostoma*
Goldfinch, Lawrence's	*Carduelis lawrencei*
Lesser	*C. psaltria*

Goose, Canada	*Branta canadensis*
Greater White-fronted	*Anser albifrons*
Ross'	*Chen rossii*
Snow	*C. caerulescens*
Gopher, Botta Pocket	*Thomomys bottae*
Goshawk, Northern	*Accipiter gentilis*
Grape, Wild	*Vitus girdiana*
Grass, Dune	*Elymus mollis*
European Beach	*Ammophila arenaria*
Melic	*Melica californica*
Salt	*Distichlis spicata*
Solano	*Tuctoria mucronata*
Triple-awned	*Aristida adcensionis*
Grebe, Eared	*Podiceps nigricollis*
Horned	*P. auritus*
Pied-billed	*Podilymbus podiceps*
Western	*Aechmophorus occidentalis*
Greenbrier	*Smilax californica*
Grosbeak, Black-headed	*Pheucticus melanocephalus*
Blue	*Guiraca caerulea*
Evening	*Coccothraustes vespertinus*
Gum Plant, Humboldt Bay	*Grindelia stricta blakei*
Hairgrass, Annual	*Deschampsia danthonoides*
Hare, Black-tailed	*Lepus californicus*
Harrier, Northern	*Circus cyaneus*
Harvestman, Blind	*Sitalcina tiburona*
Hawk, Cooper's	*Accipiter cooperi*
Ferruginous	*Buteo regalis*
Red-shouldered	*B. lineatus*
Red-tailed	*B. jamaicensis*
Rough-legged	*B. lagopus*
Sharp-shinned	*Accipiter striatus*
Swainson's	*Buteo swainsoni*
Hazardia, Island	*Hazardia detonsus*
Heath, Alkali	*Frankenia grandifolia*
Hedge Hyssop	*Gratiola heterosepala*
Hemlock, Poison	*Conium maculatum*
Heron, Black-crowned Night	*Nycticorax nycticorax*
Great Blue	*Ardea herodius*
Green-backed	*Butoroides striatus*
Honeysuckle	*Lonicera sp.*
Hopsage, Spiny	*Grayia spinosa*
Horsebrush, Mojave	*Tetradymia stenolepis*
Huckleberry, California	*Vaccinium ovatum*

Hummingbird, Anna's	*Calypte anna*
Black-chinned	*Archilochus alexandri*
Costa's	*Calypte costa*
Indigo Bush	*Dalea schottii*
Iodine Bush	*Allenrolfia occidentalis*
Iris, Douglas's	*Iris douglasiana*
Ironwood, Santa Cruz Island	*Lyonothamnus floribundus asplenifolius*
Ithuriel's Spear	*Triteleia laxa*
Jay, Blue	*Cyanocitta cristata*
Santa Cruz Island Scrub	*Aphelocoma coerulescens santacruzae*
Scrub	*A. coerulescens*
Steller's	*Cyanocitta stelleri*
Johnny Jump-up	*Viola pedunculata*
Johnny Tuck	*Orthocarpus erianthus*
Joint-fir, Nevada	*Ephedra nevadensis*
Joshua Tree	*Yucca brevifolia*
Junco, Dark-eyed	*Junco hyemalis*
Juniper, California	*Juniperus californica*
Kangaroo Rat, Giant	*Dipodomys ingens*
Heermann's	*D. heermannii*
Merriam's	*D. merriami*
San Joaquin	*D. nitritoides*
Stephens'	*D. stephensi*
Kestrel, American	*Falco sparverius*
Killdeer	*Charadrius vociferous*
Kingbird, Cassin's	*Tyrannus vociferans*
Western	*T. verticalis*
Kingsnake, Common	*Lampropeltis getulus*
Kite, Black-shouldered	*Elanus caeruleus*
Knotweed, Swamp	*Polygonum hydropiperoides*
Lark, Horned	*Eremophila alpestris*
Larkspur, Alkali	*Delphinium recurvatum*
Western	*D. hesperium*
Lichen, Reindeer	*Cladina pacifica*
Lilac, California	*Ceanothus spp.*
Lily, Adobe	*Fritillaria pluriflora*
Alkali Mariposa	*Calochortus striatus*
Fontane Star	*Zigadenus fontanus*
Tiburon Mariposa	*Calochortus tiburonensis*
Limpet, Owl	*Lottia gigantea*
Linanthus, Baldwin Lake	*Linanthus killipii*
Live-forever, Greene's	*Dudleya greenei*
Santa Cruz Island	*D. nesiotica*

Lizard, Blunt-nosed Leopard	*Gambelia silus*
California Legless	*Anniella pulchra*
Coachella Valley	
Fringe-toed	*Uma inornata*
Colorado Desert	
Fringe-toed	*U. paraphygas*
Desert Horned	*Phrynosoma platyrhinos*
Desert Night	*Xantusia vigilis*
Desert Spiny	*Sceloporis magister*
Flat-tailed Horned	*Phrynosoma m'calli*
Island Night	*Klauberina riversiana*
Long-nosed Leopard	*Gambelia wislizenii*
Mojave Fringe-toed	*Uma exsul*
Side-blotched	*Uta stansburiana*
Southern Alligator	*Gerrhonotus multicarinatus*
Western Fence	*Sceloporis occidentalis*
Zebra-tailed	*Callisaurus draconoides*
Lovevine, Indian	*Cuscuta howelliana*
Lupine, Bush	*Lupinus arboreus*
Miniature	*L. bicolor*
Madrone	*Arbutus menziesii*
Magpie, Yellow-billed	*Pica nuttalli*
Mallard	*Anas platyrhyncus*
Mallow, Mendocino Bush	*Malacothamnus mendocinensis*
Mammoth, Channel Islands	
Pygmy	*Mammuthus exilis*
Imperial	*M. imperator*
Man Root	*Marah macrocarpa*
Manzanita, Hoover's	*Arctostaphylos hooveri*
Ione	*A. myrtifolia*
Island	*A. insularis*
Maple, Big-leaf	*Acer macrophyllum*
Martin, Purple	*Progne subis*
Meadowfoam	*Limnanthes douglasiana*
Meadowlark, Western	*Sturnella neglecta*
Merganser, Common	*Mergus merganser*
Hooded	*Lohpodytes cullatus*
Merlin	*Falco columbarius*
Mesquite	*Prosopis juliflora*
Milkmaid, California	*Dentaria californica*
Mink	*Mustela vison*
Mistletoe, Desert	*Phoradendron californicum*
Mockingbird, Northern	*Mimus polyglottos*
Monkeyflower, Eyestrain	*Mimulus exiguus*

Seep-spring	*M. guttatus*
Sticky	*Diplacus longiflorus*
Moorhen, Common	*Gallinula chloropus*
Mormon Tea	*Ephedra californica*
Mountain Lion	*Felis concolor*
Mouse, Deer	*Peromyscus maniculatus*
House	*Mus musculus*
Little Pocket	*Perognathus longimembris*
Long-tailed Pocket	*P. formosus*
Salinas Harvest	*Reithrodontomys megalotis distichlis*
Salt Marsh Harvest	*R. megalotis raviventris*
San Joaquin Pocket	*Perognathus inornatus*
Southern Grasshopper	*Onychomis torridis*
Mugwort	*Artemisia douglasiana*
Mule Fat	*Baccharis glutinosa*
Mullein, Turkey	*Eremocarpus setigerus*
Muskrat	*Ondatra zibethicus*
Mustard, Slender-petaled	*Thelypodium stenopetalum*
Navarretia, Many-flowered	*Navarretia plieantha*
White-flowered	*N. leucocephala*
Needlegrass, Desert	*Stipa speciosa*
Purple	*S. pulchra*
Neostapfia	*Neostapfia, colusa*
Nettle, Stinging	*Urtica californica*
Newt, Red-bellied	*Taricha rivularis*
Rough-skinned	*T. granulosa*
Oak, California Black	*Quercus kelloggii*
Canyon Live	*Q. chrysolepis*
Coast Live	*Q. agrifolia*
Engelmann	*Q. engelmannii*
Oregon	*Q. garryana*
Scrub	*Q. dumosa*
Tanbark	*Lithocarpus densiflora*
Valley	*Quercus lobata*
Oat-grass, California Wild	*Danthonia californica*
Oats, Wild	*Avena barbata*
Opossum, Virginia	*Didelphis virginiana*
Orca	*Orcinus orca*
Orchid, Calypso	*Calypso bulbosa*
Ladies' Tresses	*Spiranthes romanzoffiana*
Phantom	*Eburophyton austinae*
Rein	*Pipera elegans*
Orcutt Grass, California	*Orcuttia californica*
Greene's	*O. greenei*

Hairy	*O. pilosa*
Slender	*O. tenuis*
Oriole, Hooded	*Icterus cucullatus*
Northern	*I. galbula*
Osprey	*Pandion haliaetus*
Otter, River	*Lutra canadensis*
Sea	*Enhydra lutris*
Ovenbird	*Seiurus aurocapillus*
Owl, Barred	*Strix varia*
Burrowing	*Athene cunicularia*
Common Barn	*Tyto alba*
Great Horned	*Bubo virginianus*
Short-eared	*Aseo flammeus*
Snowy	*Nyctea scandiaca*
Spotted	*Strix occidentalis*
Western Screech	*Otus kennicottii*
Owl's Clover, Humboldt Bay	*Orthocarpus castillejoides humboldtiensis*
Purple	*O. purpurascens*
Yellow	*O. lasiorynchus*
Paintbrush, Ash-gray	*Castilleja cinerea*
Tiburon	*C. neglecta*
Palm, California Fan	*Washingtonia filifera*
Pea, Beach	*Lathyrus maritimus*
Peewee, Greater	*Contopus pertinax*
Western Wood	*C. sordidulus*
Pelican, California Brown	*Pelecanus occidentalis*
White	*P. erythrorhynchos*
Peppergrass, Shiny	*Lepidium nitidum*
Phainopepla	*Phainopepla nitens*
Phalarope, Wilson's	*Phalaropus tricolor*
Phoebe, Black	*Sayornis nigricans*
Say's	*S. saya*
Pickleweed	*Salicornia virginica*
Pine, Beach	*Pinus contorta*
Lodgepole	*P. murrayana*
Ponderosa	*P. ponderosa*
Sugar	*P. lambertiana*
Pineapple Weed	*Matricaria matricarioides*
Pintail, Northern	*Anas acuta*
Plover, Black-bellied	*Pluvialis squatarola*
Semipalmated	*Charadrius semipalmatus*
Snowy	*C. alexandrinus*
Plum, Western	*Prunus subcordata*

Poison-oak	*Toxicodendron diversilobum*
Pondweed, Horned	*Zannichellia palustris*
Poorwill, Common	*Phalaenoptilus nuttallii*
Popcorn Flower	*Plagiobothrys sp.*
Poppy, California	*Eschscholzia californica*
Porcupine	*Erithizone dorsatum*
Primrose, Marsh	*Ludwigia peploides*
Pronghorn	*Antilocapra americana*
Quail, California	*Callipepla californica*
Gambel's	*C. gambelii*
Rabbit Brush, Common	*Chrysothamnus nauseosus*
Racer, Red	*Masticophus lateralis*
Western	*Coluber constrictor*
Raccoon	*Procyon lotor*
Rail, Black	*Laterallus jamaicensis*
California Clapper	*Rallus longirostris obsoletus*
Virginia	*R. limicola*
Rat, Dusky-footed Wood	*Neotoma fuscipes*
Rat-tails	*Ivesia argyrocoma*
Rattlesnake, Diamondback	*Crotalus atrox*
Mojave	*C. scutulatus*
Red Diamond	*C. ruber*
Western	*C. viridis*
Rattlesnake-plaintain	*Goodyera oblongifolia*
Raven, Common	*Corvus corax*
Redberry	*Rhamnus crocea*
Redbud	*Cercis occidentalis*
Redhead	*Aythya americana*
Redstart, American	*Setophaga rutica*
Redwood, Coast	*Sequoia sempervirens*
Reedgrass, Serpentine	*Calamagrostis ophitidis*
Rhubarb, Indian	*Peltiphyllum peltatum*
Ricegrass, Indian	*Oryzopsis hymenoides*
Ringtail	*Bassariscus astutus*
Roadrunner, Greater	*Geococcyx californianus*
Robin, American	*Turdus migratorius*
Rock-cress, Parish's	*Arabis parishii*
Rose, California Wild	*Rosa californica*
Wood	*R. gymnocarpa*
Rubberbrush, Terete-leaved	*Chrysothamnus teretifolia*
Rye Grass, Wild	*Elymus triticoides*
Sacaton, Alkali	*Sporobolus airoides*
Sage, Black	*Salvia mellifera*
Coastal	*Artemisia californica*

White	*Salvia apiana*
Salal	*Gaultheria shallon*
Salamander, California Slender	*Batrachoseps attenuatus*
Pacific Giant	*Dicamptodon ensatus*
Santa Cruz Long-toed	*Ambystoma macrodactylum croceum*
Shasta	*Hydromantes shastea*
Tiger	*Ambystoma tigrinum*
Salt Grass	*Distichlis spicata*
Saltbush, Common	*Atriplex polycarpa*
Lost Hills	*A. tularensis*
Mojave	*A. spinifera*
Spiny	*A. confertifolia*
Sandpaper Bush, Thurber	*Petalonyx thurberi*
Sandpiper, Least	*Calidris minutilla*
Solitary	*Tringa solitaria*
Spotted	*Actitis macularia*
Western	*Calidris mauri*
Sand-spurrey, Sticky	*Spergularia sp.*
Sand-verbena	*Abronia maritima*
Sandwort, Bear Valley	*Arenaria ursina*
Sapsucker, Red-breasted	*Sphyrapicus ruber*
Yellow-bellied	*S. varius*
Williamson's	*S. thyroides*
Savory, San Miguel	*Calamintha chandleri*
Scalebroom	*Lepidospartum squamatum*
Seal, Harbor	*Phoca vitulina*
Sedge, Clustered Field	*Carex praegracilis*
Santa Barbara	*C. barbarae*
Sequoia, Giant	*Sequoiadendron giganteum*
Shadscale	*Atriplex confertifolia*
Sheep, Bighorn	*Ovis canadensis*
Shooting Star	*Dodecatheon spp.*
Shoveler, Northern	*Anas clypeata*
Shrike, Loggerhead	*Lanius ludovicianus*
Sidewinder	*Crotalus cerastes*
Siskin, Pine	*Carduelis pinus*
Skink, Gilbert's	*Eumeces gilberti*
Skunk, Island Spotted	*Spilogale gracilis amphialus*
Spotted	*S. gracilis*
Striped	*Mephitis mephitis*
Smoke Tree, Desert	*Dalea spinosa*
Snail, Purple Olive	*Olivella biplicata*
Snake, Garter	*Thamnophis sirtalis*
Glossy	*Arizona elegans*

Gopher	*Pituophis melanoleucus*
Long-nosed	*Rhinocheilus lecontei*
Snowberry	*Symphoricarpos sp.*
Soap Plant	*Chlorogalum pomeridianum*
Soft Chess	*Bromus mollis*
Sora	*Porzana carolina*
Sparrow, Black-chinned	*Spizella atrogularis*
Grasshopper	*Ammodramus savannarum*
Sage	*Amphispiza belli*
Santa Barbara Song	*Melospiza melodia graminea*
Savannah	*Passerculus sandwichensis*
Song	*Melospiza melodia*
Spider, Black Widow	*Latrodectus hesperus*
Blind Harvestman	*Sitalcina tiburona*
Spruce, Sitka	*Picea sitchensis*
Spurge, Hoover	*Euphorbia hooveri*
Squaw Bush	*Rhus trilobata*
Squirrel, California Ground	*Otospermophilus beecheyi*
Flying	*Glaucomys sabrinus*
Mojave Ground	*Spermophilus mohavensis*
San Joaquin Antelope	*Ammospermophilus nelsoni*
Western Gray	*Sciurus griseus*
White-tailed Antelope	*Ammospermophilus leucurus*
Star Flower, Desert	*Lithofragma parviflora*
Stilt, Black-necked	*Himantopus mexicanus*
Stonefly, Golden	*Calineura californica*
Sunflower, Los Angeles	*Helianthus nuttallii parishii*
Swallow, Tree	*Tachycineta bicolor*
Violet-green	*T. thalassina*
Swan, Tundra	*Cygnus columbianus*
Swift, Vaux's	*Chaetura vauxi*
White-throated	*Aeronautes saxatalis*
Sycamore, Western	*Platanus californica*
Tanager, Western	*Piranga ludoviciana*
Tarweed, Tiburon	*Hemizonia multicaulis*
Teal, Blue-winged	*Anas discors*
Cinnamon	*A. cyanoptera*
Green-winged	*A. crecca*
Thimbleberry	*Rubus parviflorus*
Thistle, Milk	*Silybum marianum*
Thrasher, California	*Toxostoma redivivum*
Le Conte's	*T. lecontei*
Sage	*Oreoscoptes montanus*
Thrush, Hermit	*Catharus guttatus*

Timothy, Swamp	*Phleum pratense*
Titmouse, Plain	*Parus inornatus*
Toad, Spade-foot	*Scaphiopus hammondi*
Tortoise, Desert	*Hydrobates agassizi*
Towhee, Brown	*Pipilo fuscus*
Rufous-sided	*P. erythrothalmus*
Toyon	*Heteromeles arbutifolia*
Trillium, Giant	*Trillium giganteum*
Trout, Brown	*Salmo trutta*
Eastern Brook	*Salvelinus fontinalis*
Lake	*S. namaycush*
Shasta Rainbow	*Salmo gairdnerii shastensis*
Tryonia imitator	*Tryonia imitator*
Tule	*Scirpus spp.*
Tule Potato	*Sagittaria latifolia*
Tulip, Oakland Star	*Calochortus umbellatus*
Turtle, Western Pond	*Clemmys marmorata*
Verdin	*Auriparus flaviceps*
Violet, Yellow	*Viola lobata*
Vireo, Least Bell's	*Vireo bellii pusillus*
Red-eyed	*V. olivaceus*
Solitary	*V. solitarius*
Warbling	*V. gilvus*
Virgin's Bower	*Clematis ligusticifolia*
Vole, Red Tree	*Arborimus longicaudus*
Vulture, Turkey	*Cathartes aura*
Wallflower, Menzies'	*Erysimum menziesii*
Wapatoo	*Sagittaria latifolia*
Warbler, Bay-breasted	*Dendroica castanea*
Blackburnian	*D. fusca*
Black-throated Blue	*D. caerulescens*
Black-throated Gray	*D. nigrescens*
Canada	*Wilsonia canadensis*
Cape May	*Dendroica tigrina*
MacGillivray's	*Oporornis tolmiei*
Nashville	*Vermivora ruficapilla*
Northern Parula	*Parula americana*
Orange-crowned	*Vermivora celata*
Red-faced	*Cardellina rubifroms*
Tennessee	*Vermivora peregrina*
Townsend's	*Dendroica townsendii*
Wilson's	*Wilsonia pusilla*
Yellow-rumped	*Dendroica coronata*
Yellow	*D. petechia*

Watercress	*Coronopus didymos*
Watershield	*Brasenia schreberi*
Weasel, Long-tailed	*Mustela frenata*
Whale, California Gray	*Eschrichtius robustus*
Whimbrel	*Numenius phaeopus*
Whipsnake, Western	*Masticophus taeniatus*
Whiptail, Western	*Cnemidophorus tigris*
Whitethorn	*Ceanothus icanus*
Wigeon, American	*Anas americana*
Wildrye, Creeping	*Elymus triticoides*
Willet	*Cataptrophorus semipalmatus*
Willow, Arroyo	*Salix lasiolepis*
Black	*S. gooddingii*
Red	*S. lasiandra*
Sandbar	*S. hindsiana*
Slender	*S. exigua*
Winterfat	*Eurotia lanata*
Wintergreen, White-veined	*Pyrolia picta*
Witch-grass, Western	*Panicum barbipulvinatum*
Woodland Star	*Zigadenus fremontii*
Woodpecker, Acorn	*Melanerpes formicivorus*
Downy	*Picoides pubescens*
Hairy	*P. villosus*
Ladder-backed	*P. scalaris*
Lewis's	*Melanerpes lewis*
Nuttall's	*Picoides nuttallii*
Pileated	*Drycopus pileatus*
Wolf, Cascades Gray	*Canis lupus*
Wolverine	*Gulo gulo*
Wren, Bewick's	*Thryomanes bewickii*
Cactus	*Campylorthunchus brunneicapillus*
House	*Troglodytes aedon*
Marsh	*Cistothorus palustris*
San Clemente Bewick's	*Thryomanes bewickii clementae*
Yarrow, Common	*Achillea millefolium*
Yellowlegs, Greater	*Tringa melanoleuca*
Yellowthroat, Common	*Geothlypis trichas*
Yerba Mansa	*Anemopsis californica*
Yew, Western	*Taxus brevifolia*
Yucca, Mojave	*Yucca schidigera*
Yucca	*Y. brevifolia*

Index